KU-004-377

easy crochet
Vintage & Retro

30 projects to make for your home and to wear

Consultant: Nikki Trench

hamlyn

An Hachette UK Company
www.hachette.co.uk

First published in Great Britain in 2013 by
Hamlyn, a division of Octopus Publishing Group Ltd
Endeavour House
189 Shaftesbury Avenue
London
WC2H 8JY
www.octopusbooks.co.uk

Copyright © Octopus Publishing Group Ltd 2013
Text and photography © Hachette Partworks Ltd 2013

All rights reserved. No part of this work may be reproduced
or utilized in any form or by any means, electronic or
mechanical, including photocopying, recording or by any
information storage and retrieval system, without the prior
written permission of the publisher.

ISBN 978-0-600-62834-7

A CIP catalogue record for this book is available from the
British Library

Printed and bound in China

10 9 8 7 6 5 4 3 2 1

easy crochet
Vintage & Retro

467 340 61 4

Contents

Introduction

Crochet is easy, and it grows fast. Master a few basic stitches (and the terminology) and you can create stylish crocheted items to wear, use to decorate your home and to give as gifts for friends and family in next to no time and with minimal experience.

Whether you are a relative beginner, a confident convert or a long-term aficionado, there are projects here to delight. While your first attempts may be a bit uneven, a little practice and experimentation will ensure you soon improve. None of the projects in this book is beyond the scope of even those fairly new to the hobby. Even the most basic of stitches can be translated into covetable items.

Crochet lends itself to the styles of a bygone age when mass-produced fashion was not an option. The timeless classics in this book range from stylish items you can wear – elegant gloves, sweaters and hats (not forgetting accessories and adornments like cuffs, collars and bags) – through to items for the home such as cushions and throws. All would make charming, unique gifts.

Crochet essentials

All you really need to get crocheting is a hook and some yarn. For many projects that's it, and where additional items are required, most of these can be found in a fairly basic sewing kit. All measurements are given in metric and imperial. Choose which to work in and stick with it since conversions may not be exact in all instances.

- **Hooks** These are sized in mm (with 'old UK' sizes given as well) and can be made from wood, plastic, aluminium, bamboo or steel. The material affects the weight and 'feel' of the hook, and which you choose is largely down to personal preference.
- **Yarns** Specific yarns are given for each project, but if you want to make substitutions, full details of the yarn's composition and the ball lengths are given so that you can choose alternatives, either from the wide range of online sources, or from your local supplier, many of whom have very knowledgeable staff. Do keep any leftover yarns (not forgetting the ball bands, since these contain vital information) to use for future projects.
- **Additional items** Some of the projects require making up and finishing, and need further materials and equipment, such as needles (both ordinary and round-pointed tapestry ones) and thread, buttons, ribbons and other accessories. These are detailed for each project in the Getting Started box.

What is in this book

All projects are illustrated with several photographs to show you the detail of the work – both inspirational and useful for reference. A full summary of each project is given in the Getting Started box so you can see exactly what's involved. Here, projects are graded from one star (straightforward, suitable for beginners) through two (more challenging) to three stars (for crocheters with more confidence and experience).

Also in the Getting Started box is the size of each finished item, yarn(s) and additional materials needed, and what tension the project is worked in. Finally, a breakdown of the steps involved is given so you know exactly what the project entails before you start.

At the start of the pattern instructions is a key to all abbreviations particular to the project and occasional notes expand on the instructions if necessary.

Additional information

Occasionally, more information or a specialist technique is needed. How To boxes, diagrams and keys clarify these potentially tricky steps. The box on page 19, for example, explains how to work the furry cuffs, while on page 23 a detailed diagram shows the exact measurements for the slip for the sixties-style dress.

If you have enjoyed the projects here, you may want to explore the other titles in the Easy Crochet series: *Babies & Children, Country, Flowers, Seaside* and *Weekend*. For those who enjoy knitting, a sister series, Easy Knitting, features similarly stylish yet simple projects.

Jacket with bow waist

The demure styling of this jacket is perfect when teamed with a floaty skirt or dress.

This neat fitted jacket has a small collar and three-quarter length sleeves. Its waist is emphasized with a crochet belt featuring a bow trim at the front.

The Yarn
Sirdar Calico DK (approx. 158m/172 yards per 50g/1¾oz ball) is a blend of 60% cotton and 40% acrylic. It makes an attractive lightweight machine-washable cotton fabric. There is a good range of natural shades with some bright contemporary colours.

GETTING STARTED

★★ *Easy stitch pattern but this garment requires quite a lot of shaping.*

Size:
To fit bust: 81[86:91:97]cm (32[34:36:38]in)
Actual size: 88.5[93.5:98.5:103.5]cm (35[36¾:38¾:40¾]in)
Length: 55[55:57:57]cm (21½[21½:22½:22½]in)
Sleeve seam: 30cm (12in)
Note: Figures in square brackets [ ] refer to larger sizes; where there is only one set of figures, it applies to all sizes

How much yarn:
8[9:10:11] x 50g (1¾oz) balls of Sirdar Calico DK in Linen (shade 721)

Hooks:
3.50mm (UK 9) crochet hook
4.00mm (UK 8) crochet hook

Additional items:
5 buttons
2 press fasteners

Tension:
8 Vs (1htr, 1ch, 1htr) and 13 rows measure 10cm (4in) square on 4.00mm (UK 8) hook
IT IS ESSENTIAL TO WORK TO THE STATED TENSION TO ACHIEVE SUCCESS

What you have to do:
Work throughout in V-stitch pattern, shaping for waist, armholes and neckline as directed. Work front edgings, collar and belt in double crochet.

 # Instructions

BACK:
With 4.00mm (UK 8) hook make 72[76:80:84]ch.
Foundation row: (RS) 1htr, 1ch and 1htr all into 4th ch from hook, *miss next ch, work 1htr, 1ch and 1htr all into next ch (V formed), rep from * to last 2ch, miss next ch, 1htr into last ch, turn. 34[36:38:40] Vs.
Patt row: 2ch (counts as first htr), work 1 V into each V to last htr, 1htr into last htr, turn. The last row forms patt. Cont in patt until work measures 18cm (7in) from beg, ending with a WS row.

Shape for waist:
**Next row: 2ch, (2htr into next V) to last htr, 1htr into last htr, turn.
Next row: 2ch, (2htr between next 2htr) to last htr, 1htr into last htr, turn. Rep last row 4 times more.
Next row: 2ch, (work 1 V between next 2htr) to last htr, 1htr into last htr, turn. 34[36:38:40] Vs.
Cont in patt until work measures 36cm (14in) from beg, ending a WS row.**
Shape armholes:
1st row: Ss over first htr and 2 Vs and into next V, 2ch,

Abbreviations:

beg = beginning
ch = chain(s)
cm = centimetre(s)
cont = continue
dc = double crochet
dec = decrease
htr = half treble
inc = increase
patt = pattern
rep = repeat
RS = right side
ss = slip stitch
st(s) = stitch(es)
WS = wrong side

patt to last 3 Vs, 1htr into next V, turn. 28[30:32:34] Vs.

2nd row: Patt to end, turn.

3rd row: 2ch, 1htr into first V, patt to last V and htr, 1htr into last V, 1htr in last htr, turn.

4th row: 2ch, miss next htr, patt to last 2htr, miss next htr, 1htr into last htr, turn. 26[28:30:32] Vs. Rep last 2 rows twice more. 22[24:26:28] Vs. Cont without shaping until armholes measure 19[19:21:21]cm (7½[7½:8¼:8¼]in), ending with a WS row.

Shape shoulders:

Next row: Ss over first htr and 2[3:3:3] Vs and into next V, 2ch, patt to last 3[4:4:4] Vs, 1htr into next V, turn. 16[16:18:20] Vs.

Next row: Ss over first htr and 2[2:2:3] Vs and into next V, 2ch, patt to last 3[3:3:4] Vs, 1htr into next V. 10[10:12:12] Vs. Fasten off.

LEFT FRONT:

With 4.00mm (UK 8) hook make 40[42:44:46]ch. Work foundation row and patt

row as given for Back. 18[19:20:21] Vs. Cont in patt until work measures 18cm (7in) from beg, ending with a WS row.

Shape for waist:
Work as given for Back from ** to **.

Shape armhole:

1st row: Ss over first htr and 2 Vs and into next V, patt to end, turn. 15[16:17:18] Vs.

2nd row: Patt to end, turn.

3rd row: 2ch, 1htr into first V, patt to end, turn.

4th row: Patt to last 2htr, miss next htr, 1htr into last htr, turn. 14[15:16:17] Vs. Rep last 2 rows twice more. 12[13:14:15] Vs. Cont without shaping until armhole measures 12[12:14:14]cm (4¾[4¾:5½:5½]in), ending at front edge.

Shape neck:

1st row: (WS) Ss over first htr and 2[2:3:3] Vs and into next V, 2ch, patt to end, turn. 9[10:10:11] Vs.

2nd row: Patt to end, turn.

3rd row: 2ch, 1htr into first V, patt to end, turn.

4th row: Patt to last 2htr, miss next htr, 1htr into last htr, turn. 8[9:9:10] Vs. Rep last 2 rows twice more. 6[7:7:8] Vs. Cont without shaping until armhole measures same as Back to shoulder, ending at armhole edge.

Shape shoulder:
Next row: Ss over first htr and 2[3:3:3] Vs and into next V, 2ch, patt to end. Fasten off.

RIGHT FRONT:
Work as given for Left front to armhole, so ending with a WS row.

Shape armhole:
1st row: Patt to last 3 Vs, 1htr into next V, turn. 15[16:17:18] Vs.
2nd row: Patt to end, turn.
3rd row: Patt to last V, 1htr into last V, 1htr into last htr, turn.
4th row: 2ch, miss next htr, patt to end, turn. 14[15:16:17] Vs. Rep last 2 rows twice more. 12[13:14:15] Vs. Cont without shaping until armhole measures 12[12:14:14]cm (4¾[4¾:5½:5½]in), ending at armhole edge.

Shape neck:
1st row: (WS) Patt to last 3[3:4:4] Vs, 1htr into next V, turn. 9[10:10:11] Vs.
2nd row: Patt to end, turn.
3rd row: Patt to last V, 1htr into last V, 1htr into last htr, turn.
4th row: 2ch, miss next htr, patt to end, turn. 8[9:9:10] Vs. Rep last 2 rows twice more. 6[7:7:8] Vs. Cont without shaping until armhole measures same as Back to shoulder, ending at neck edge.

Shape shoulder:
Next row: Patt to last 3[4:4:4] Vs, 1htr into next V. Fasten off.

SLEEVES: (make 2)
With 4.00mm (UK 8) hook make 40[40:46:46]ch. Work foundation row and patt row as given for Back. 18[18:21:21] Vs. Patt 2 more rows.
1st inc row: 2ch, 1htr into first htr, patt to last htr, 2htr into last htr, turn.
2nd inc row: 2ch, 1 V between first 2htr, patt to last 2htr, 1 V between last 2htr, 1htr into last htr, turn. 20[20:23:23] Vs. Patt 4 rows. Rep last 6 rows 3 times more, then work 2 inc rows again. 28[28:31:31] Vs. Cont without shaping until Sleeve measures 30cm (12in), ending with a WS row.

Shape top:
1st row: Ss over first htr and 2 Vs and into next V, 2ch, patt to last 3 Vs, 1htr into next V, turn. 22[22:25:25] Vs.
2nd row: 2ch, 1htr into first V, patt to last V and htr, 1htr into last V, 1htr in last htr, turn.
3rd row: 2ch, miss next htr, patt to last 2htr, miss next htr, 1htr into last htr, turn. 20[20:23:23] Vs. Rep last 2 rows 4[4:5:5] times more (12[12:15:15] Vs), then work first of these 2 rows again. Fasten off.

BUTTON BAND:
Join shoulder seams.
With 3.50mm (UK 9) hook and RS of work facing, join on yarn and work a row of dc evenly along Left front edge, working 3dc into every 2 row-ends. Work 2 more rows dc. Fasten off. Mark 5 button positions on band, the first 1cm (⅜in) from neck edge, the last 1cm (⅜in) below waist and the others evenly spaced between.

BUTTONHOLE BAND AND COLLAR:
With 3.50mm (UK 9) hook and RS of work facing, join on yarn and work a row of dc evenly along Right front edge, turn.
1st buttonhole row: Work in dc to end, working buttonholes to correspond with markers by working 2ch and missing 2dc.
2nd buttonhole row: Work in dc, working 2dc into each ch space. Do not turn but work collar as follows:

Collar:
Work 1dc into each row-end of buttonhole band, then work 20dc evenly up right front neck, 21[21:25:25]dc across back neck, 20dc evenly down left front neck and 1dc into each row-end of button band, turn. 67[67:71:71] dc. Work 3 rows dc. Change to 4.00mm (UK 8) hook and cont in dc until collar measures 6.5cm (2½in). Fasten off.

BELT:
With 4.00mm (UK 8) hook make 173[181:189:197]ch.
Foundation row: (WS) 1dc into 2nd ch from hook, 1dc into each ch to end, turn. Work 6 rows dc. Fasten off.

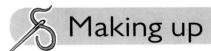 Making up

Set in sleeves, then join side and sleeve seams. Sew on buttons to correspond with buttonholes. Fold fabric to form a 10cm (4in) wide bow at right end of belt. Gather centre of bow with a length of chain. Sew one half of each press fastener on WS of belt, level with each side of bow, then sew other half to RS of opposite end of belt to fasten.

Vintage-style throw

Work a Seventies vibe with this amazing retro throw.

With its striking colouring and Seventies-style chevron striped pattern, this throw in a soft cotton yarn as real retro appeal.

GETTING STARTED

Chevron pattern requires concentration to start but becomes straightforward as you progress.

Size:
115 x 98cm (45 x 38½in)

How much yarn:
2 x 100g (3½oz) balls of King Cole Bamboo Cotton DK in each of six colours: A – Navy (shade 542); B – Opal (shade 527); C – Aqua (shade 576); D – Mint (shade 517); E – Shrimp (shade 535) and F – Moss (shade 526)

Hook:
7.00mm (UK 2) crochet hook

Tension:
1 patt rep measures 16.5cm (6½in) and 6 rows measure 14cm (5½in) over patt on 7.00mm (UK 2) hook using yarn double
IT IS ESSENTIAL TO WORK TO THE STATED TENSION TO ACHIEVE SUCCESS

What you have to do:
Work throughout in trebles and chevron pattern, increasing and decreasing stitches to form pattern as directed. Use six colours and double yarn to work single-row stripes, working each row from right side.

The Yarn
King Cole Bamboo Cotton DK (approx. 230m/251 yards per 100g/3½oz ball) contains 50% bamboo and 50% cotton. This soft, natural yarn is easy to work with and is available in a wide range of shades.

Instructions

Abbreviations:

ch = chain(s)

cm = centimetre(s)

patt = pattern

rep = repeat

RS = right side

sp = space

st(s) = stitch(es)

tr = treble

yrh = yarn round hook

THROW:

With 7.00mm (UK 2) hook and 2 strands of A, make 180ch.

Foundation row: (RS) 1tr into 4th ch from hook, (miss 1ch, 2tr into next ch) 4 times, *miss 1ch, (2tr, 2ch, 2tr) into next ch, (miss 1ch, 2tr into next ch) 5 times, (miss 1ch, yrh, insert hook into next ch, yrh and draw a loop through) twice, yrh and draw through all 5 loops on hook, (miss 1ch, 2tr into next ch) 5 times, rep from * 5 times more, miss 1ch, (2tr, 2ch, 2tr) into next ch, (miss 1ch, 2tr into next ch) 5 times. Fasten off.

Patt row: With RS facing, join 2 strands of B between 3rd and 4th sts of previous row (counting turning ch as first st), 3ch (counts as first tr), 1tr into same sp, (2tr between next pair of tr) 4 times, *(2tr, 2ch, 2tr) into 2ch sp, (2tr between next pair of tr) 5 times, (yrh, insert hook between next pair of tr, yrh and draw a loop through) twice, yrh and draw through all 5 loops on hook, (2tr between next pair of tr) 5 times, rep from * 5 times more, (2tr, 2ch, 2tr) into 2ch sp, (2tr between next pair of tr) 5 times. Fasten off. Work 4 more rows in patt, working 1 row in each in C, D, E and F. The last 6 rows form patt and colour sequence. Rep them 6 times more to complete throw. Fasten off.

Fabulous furry cuffs

A quick and easy way to add a touch of luxe to an otherwise plain jacket or coat.

Simulate the look of luxurious fur by trimming the sleeves of a coat or jacket with these cuffs of fake fur. Worked in trebles throughout, they are straightforward to make and sew in place.

GETTING STARTED

★★ *Not difficult but working with textured yarn requires patience.*

Size:
7 x 30cm (2¾ x 12in)

How much yarn:
1 x 50g (1¾oz) ball of Sirdar Funky Fur in Walnut (shade 549)

Additional items:
Matching sewing thread and needle

Hook:
4.00mm (UK 8) crochet hook

Tension:
14 sts and 10 rows measure 10cm (4in) square over tr on 4.00mm (UK 8) hook
IT IS ESSENTIAL TO WORK TO THE STATED TENSION TO ACHIEVE SUCCESS

What you have to do:
Make foundation chain for seam edge of cuff. Work throughout in trebles, working into space between trebles and not into actual stitches. Sew cuffs in place on jacket sleeves.

The Yarn
Sirdar Funky Fur (approx. 90m/98 yards per 50g/1¾oz ball) is 100% polyester. It is a novelty yarn with 'eyelash' fibres that resemble fur when worked. As well as natural shades, there are also several fun brighter shades.

Instructions

Abbreviations:

beg = beginning
ch = chain(s)
cm = centimetre(s)
rep = repeat
sp = space
st(s) = stitch(es)
tr = treble(s)

Note:

Working with heavily textured yarn can be difficult to start with as you cannot see the stitches clearly, but you will soon get used to crocheting in a different way. The foundation row of trebles is worked into one loop of each of the foundation chains. Subsequent rows of trebles are worked into the spaces between the stitches in the previous row. Use your fingers to feel the space as you work.

CUFFS: (make 2)

With 4.00mm (UK 8) hook make 11ch.

Foundation row: 1tr into 4th ch from hook, 1tr into each ch to end, turn. 9 sts.

1st row: 3ch (counts as first tr), *1tr into next sp between tr, rep from * to end, working last tr into sp between last tr and turning ch, turn. 9 sts. Rep last row throughout until work measures 30cm (12in) (or length required) from beg. Fasten off.

Making up

Using matching sewing thread slip stitch two short ends of cuff together.

Slide cuff over end of sleeve so that cuff seam lines up with sleeve seam.

Pin in place, making sure that lower edge of cuff sits evenly along hem of sleeve, then slip stitch in position.

HOW TO
WORK THE CUFFS

Crocheting with a textured yarn, such as this eyelash yarn, takes a little practice and here the treble crochet is worked in a slightly different way to accommodate this.

1 Make a foundation chain of eleven chains. On the foundation row, work one treble into the fourth chain from the hook and one treble into each chain to the end. Work each treble into one loop of the foundation chain. Turn the work

2 Make a turning chain of three chains, this counts as the first treble. Use the tip of your index finger on the left hand to locate the next space between the trebles on the row below.

3 Work a treble into this space and into each space between trebles to the end of the row, working the last treble into the space between the last treble and the turning chain. Check that you have nine stitches and turn the work.

4 Continue repeating the first row until the cuff is the required length and fasten off.

Sixties-style shift

Work a retro look with this neat tunic, which recalls the days of Twiggy and the twist.

Take a fresh look at Sixties styling with this scoop-neck, openwork shift. Its yoke and short sleeves are worked in trebles, while there are instructions to sew a simple slip to wear underneath the shift.

GETTING STARTED

★★ *Pattern is straightforward to follow once you get started.*

Size:

To fit bust: 81[86:91]cm (32[34:36]in)

Actual size: 87[93:99]cm (34¼[36½:39]in)

Length: 77[78:79]cm (30¼[30¾:31]in)

Sleeve seam: 8[10:10]cm (3¼[4:4]in)

Note: Figures in square brackets [ ] refer to larger sizes; where there is only one set of figures, it applies to all sizes

How much yarn:

13[14:16] x 50g (1¾oz) balls of Sirdar Juicy DK in Coconut Milk (shade 428)

Hooks:

3.50mm (UK 9) crochet hook

4.00mm (UK 8) crochet hook

Additional items:

80cm (⅞ yard) of 140cm-wide cotton lawn in white

90[90:100]cm (1[1:1⅛] yard) of 1cm (⅜in) wide white ribbon

White sewing thread and sewing needle

Press fastener

Tension:

4 patt repeats measure 10cm (4in) square; 17tr and 10 rows measure 10cm (4in) square on 3.50mm (UK9) hook

IT IS ESSENTIAL TO WORK TO THE STATED TENSION TO ACHIEVE SUCCESS

What you have to do:

Work main (openwork) pattern in double crochet and chain loops. Change hook sizes to shape body of tunic. Work yoke and sleeves in trebles. Shape armholes, neckline and sleeves as directed. Work double crochet edging around neckline.

The Yarn

Sirdar Juicy DK (approx. 95m/104 yards per 50g/1¾oz ball) is a blend of 80% bamboo sourced viscose and 20% cotton that can be machine washed. It makes a comfortable fabric with a silky feel and slight sheen. The colour palette includes mainly pastel shades.

 # Instructions

BACK:

With 4.00mm (UK 8) hook make 92[97:102]ch.

1st foundation row: (RS) 1dc into 2nd ch from hook, 1dc into each ch to end, turn.

2nd foundation row: 1ch (does not count as a st), 1dc into each of first 2dc, *5ch, miss next 2dc, 1dc into each of next 3dc, rep from * to end, finishing last rep with 1dc

Abbreviations:

beg = beginning
ch = chain
cm = centimetre(s)
cont = continue
dc = double crochet
dec = decreased
dtr = double treble
foll = follows
inc = increased
patt = pattern
rep = repeat
RS = right side
sp = space
ss = slip stitch
st(s) = stitch(es)
tog = together
tr = treble
tr2tog = into each of next 2 sts work (yrh, insert hook into st, yrh and draw a loop through, yrh and draw through first two loops on hook), yrh and draw through all 3 loops left on hook
WS = wrong side
yrh = yarn round hook

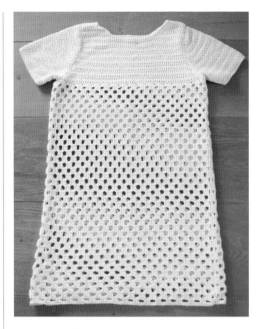

into each of last 2dc, turn. 18[19:20] loops. Cont in patt as foll:

1st row: 1ch, 1dc into first dc, *5dc all into next loop, miss next dc, 1dc into next dc, rep from * to end, turn.

2nd row: 6ch (counts as 1dtr and 2ch), miss first 2dc, 1dc into each of next 3dc, *5ch, miss next 3dc, 1dc into each of next 3dc, rep from * to last 2dc, 2ch, 1dtr into last dc, turn.

3rd row: 1ch, 1dc into first dtr, 2dc into next 2ch sp, miss next dc, 1dc into next dc, *5dc all into next loop, miss next dc, 1dc into next dc, rep from * to last 2ch sp, 2dc into last sp, 1dc into 4th of 6ch, turn.

4th row: 1ch, 1dc into each of first 2dc, *5ch, miss next 3dc, 1dc into each of next 3dc, rep from * to end, finishing last rep with 1dc into each of last 2dc, turn. These 4 rows form patt. Cont in patt until work measures 40cm (16in) from beg, ending with a WS row. Change to 3.50mm (UK 9) hook. Cont in patt until work measures 56cm (22in) from beg, ending with a 1st row.

Next row: 5ch, miss first 2dc, 1dc into each of next 3dc, *4ch,

miss next 3dc, 1dc into each of next 3dc, rep from * to last 2dc, 1ch, 1dtr into last dc, turn.

Yoke:

Next row: 3ch (counts as first tr), 1tr into first ch sp, 1tr into next dc, tr2tog, *2tr into next loop, 1tr into next dc, tr2tog, rep from * to last ch sp, 1tr into last sp, 1tr into 4th of 5ch, turn. 74[78:82]tr.

Next row: 3ch, miss st at base of ch, 1tr into each tr to end, turn. Cont in tr as foll:

Shape armholes:

Next row: Ss into each of first 7tr, 3ch, miss st at base of ch, 1tr into each tr to last 6tr, turn.

Next row: 3ch, miss st at base of ch, tr2tog, 1tr into each tr to last 3 sts, tr2tog, 1tr into 3rd of 3ch, turn.
Rep last row 3[4:5] times more. 54[56:58] tr. Cont without shaping until armholes measure 14[15:16]cm (5½[6:6¼]in) from beg, ending with a WS row.

Shape neck:

Next row: 3ch, miss st at base of ch, 1tr into each of next 12[13:14]tr, (tr2tog) twice, 1tr into next tr, turn. 16[17:18]tr. Work on first side of neck as foll:

1st row: 3ch, miss st at base of ch, (tr2tog) twice, 1tr into each tr to end, working last tr into 3rd of 3ch, turn.

2nd row: 3ch, miss st at base of ch, 1tr into each tr to last 5 sts, (tr2tog) twice, 1tr into 3rd of 3ch, turn.

3rd row: As 1st row.

4th row: 3ch, miss st at base of ch, 1tr into each st to end. 10[11:12]tr. Fasten off. With RS of work facing, miss next 18tr at base of neck, join yarn to next tr, 3ch, miss st at base of ch, (tr2tog) twice, 1tr into each tr to end, working last tr into 3rd of 3ch, turn. 16[17:18]tr.

1st row: 3ch, miss st at base of ch, 1tr into each tr to last 5 sts, (tr2tog) twice, 1tr into 3rd of 3ch, turn.

2nd row: 3ch, miss st at base of ch, (tr2tog) twice, 1tr into each tr to end, working last tr into 3rd of 3ch, turn.

3rd row: As 1st row.

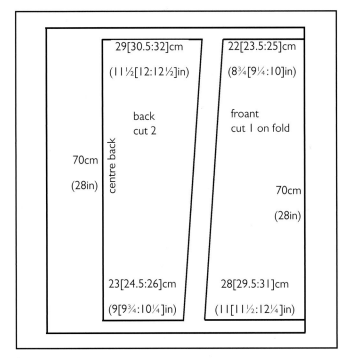

Diagram showing:
- back cut 2: 29[30.5:32]cm (11½[12:12½]in), 23[24.5:26]cm (9[9¾:10¼]in), centre back, 70cm (28in)
- froant cut 1 on fold: 22[23.5:25]cm (8¾[9¼:10]in), 28[29.5:31]cm (11[11½:12¼]in), 70cm (28in)

4th row: 3ch, miss st at base of ch, 1tr into each st to end. Fasten off.

FRONT:
Work as given for Back.

SLEEVES: (make 2)
With 3.50mm (UK 9) hook make 56[60:62]ch.
Foundation row: (RS) 1tr into 4th ch from hook, 1tr into each ch to end, turn. 54[58:60]tr.
Inc row: 3ch (counts as first tr), 1tr into st at base of ch, 1tr into each tr to last st, 2tr into 3rd of 3ch, turn. 2tr increased.
Next row: 3ch, miss st at base of ch, 1tr into each tr to end, working last tr into 3rd of 3ch, turn. Rep last 2 rows 2[3:3] times more, then work inc row again. 62[68:70]tr.
Shape top:
Next row: Ss into each of first 7tr, 3ch, miss st at base of ch, 1tr into each tr to last 6tr, turn.
Next row: 3ch, miss st at base of ch, (tr2tog) twice, 1tr into each tr to last 5 sts, (tr2tog) twice, 1tr into 3rd of 3ch, turn. 4tr decreased.
Next row: 3ch, miss st at base of ch, tr2tog, 1tr into each tr to last 3 sts, tr2tog, 1tr into 3rd of 3ch, turn. 2tr decreased. Rep last 2 rows 4[5:5] times more. 20[20:22]tr. Fasten off.

 # Making up

Pin pieces to size, spray with clean water and leave until completely dry. Join shoulder seams.
Neck edging:
Join yarn to one shoulder seam and, with 3.50mm (UK 9) hook, work a row of dc evenly all round neck edge, join with a ss into first dc. Fasten off. Sew in sleeves, then join side and sleeve seams. Press seams lightly.
Slip:
Following measurements on diagram, cut one front and two back pieces. Pin the two back pieces, with RS facing. Beginning 18cm (7in) from top edge and taking 1cm (⅜in) seam allowance, join centre back seam. Pin the front to back, with RS facing. Taking 1cm (⅜in) seam allowance, join seams, leaving 10cm (4in) open at top of right side seam. Press seams open and then press 1cm (⅜in) to WS at each side of opening. Press 1cm (⅜in) to WS around top edge, then press and pin 2.5cm to WS to form a double hem.
Mark 8cm (3in) from each side seam on back and front with pins. Cut ribbon in half and insert one end of each length under pressed hem on front, at the marker. Pin in place. Repeat with other end of each ribbon, pinning in position on back. Carefully try on slip and adjust length of ribbon straps if necessary.
With ribbon straps hanging down, stitch close to inner fold, catching in ribbon and raw edge of hem. Fold ribbon up over the hem and pin. Stitch 1cm (⅜in) from top fold around entire top edge, so securing the ribbon.
Turn up double hem to correct length and stitch 1cm (⅜in) from inner fold. Press. Sew a press fastener to top of back opening.

Elegant mesh gloves

Bring some old-fashioned glamour into your life with these pretty openwork gloves.

Sophisticated in fine black cotton, these gloves are worked in a traditional filet mesh pattern and trimmed at the wrist with a pretty border featuring a buttoned opening for ease of fit.

The Yarn

Twilleys Lyscordet (approx. 200m/218 yards per 50g/1¾oz ball) contains 100% mercerised cotton in a three-ply weight. It is a traditional crochet cotton with a distinctive twist, in a good range of pastel and dark shades.

GETTING STARTED

Working with fine yarn and small hook requires patience and gloves need a lot of shaping.

Size:

To fit: *an average woman's hand*

Length from wrist to middle fingertip: *18cm (7in)*

To fit around palm: *19cm (7½in)*

How much yarn:

1 x 50g (1¾oz) ball of Twilleys Lyscordet in Black (shade 79)

Hook:

2.50mm (UK 12) crochet hook

Additional items:

2 small buttons

Tension:

13 mesh sps and 14 rows measure 10cm (4in) square over patt (when stretched in use) on 2.50mm (UK 12) hook

IT IS ESSENTIAL TO WORK TO THE STATED TENSION TO ACHIEVE SUCCESS

What you have to do:

Starting at wrist, work filet mesh pattern in rounds, leaving slit opening at inner wrist. Shape thumb gusset. Work fingers in mesh pattern in rounds. Decorate wrist edge with a frill of looped shell patterns.

Instructions

Abbreviations:
beg = beginning
ch = chain(s)
cm = centimetre(s)
dc = double crochet
dc2(3)tog = work 1dc into each of next 2(3) sts leaving last loop of each on hook, yrh and draw through all 3(4) loops
foll = follow(s)(ing)
patt = pattern
rep = repeat
RS = right side
sp(s) = space(s)
ss = slip stitch
st(s) = stitch(es)
tog = together
tr = treble(s)
tr2(3)tog = work 1tr into each of next 2(3) sts leaving last loop of each on hook, yrh and draw through all 3(4) loops
WS = wrong side
yrh = yarn round hook

LEFT GLOVE:
With 2.50mm (UK 12) hook make 50ch and beg at wrist.

1st row: (RS) 1tr in 6th ch from hook, *1ch, miss 1ch, 1tr in next ch *, rep from * to * to end. 23 mesh sps. Now join work into a round as foll, forming the top of button opening:

1st round: Do not turn the work, 4ch (counts as 1tr and 1ch), form 1st row into a circle without twisting so RS of 1st row is facing, work 1tr in 5th of 6ch at beg 1st row, 1ch, miss 1ch, * 1tr in tr, 1ch, miss 1ch*, rep from * to * ending with 1ss in 3rd of 4ch at beg of round. Fasten off. 24 mesh sps.
Foll rounds beg and end at edge of palm, opposite thumb.

Shape thumb gusset:
** Rejoin yarn to 20th tr of previous round.

1st thumb round: 4ch, miss 1ch, (1tr in tr, 1ch, miss 1ch) 9 times, (1tr, 1ch) twice in next tr, (1tr in tr, 1ch, miss 1ch) 13 times, join with a ss in 3rd of 4ch.

2nd thumb round: 4ch, miss 1ch, (1tr in tr, 1ch, miss 1ch) 9 times, (1tr, 1ch) twice in each of next 2tr, (1tr in tr, 1ch, miss 1ch) 13 times, join with a ss in 3rd of 4ch.

3rd thumb round: 4ch, miss 1ch, (1tr in tr, 1ch, miss 1ch) 9 times, (1tr, 1ch) twice in next tr, (1tr in tr, 1ch, miss 1ch) twice, (1tr, 1ch) twice in next tr, (1tr in tr, 1ch, miss 1ch) 13 times, join with a ss in 3rd of 4ch.

4th thumb round: 4ch, miss 1ch, (1tr in tr, 1ch, miss 1ch) 9 times, (1tr, 1ch) twice in next tr, (1tr in tr, 1ch, miss 1ch) 4 times, (1tr, 1ch) twice in next tr, (1tr in tr, 1ch, miss 1ch) 13 times, join with a ss in 3rd of 4ch.

5th thumb round: 4ch, miss 1ch, (1tr in tr, 1ch, miss 1ch) 9 times, (1tr, 1ch) twice in next tr, (1tr in tr, 1ch, miss 1ch) 6 times, (1tr, 1ch) twice in next tr, (1tr in tr, 1ch, miss 1ch) 13 times, join with a ss in 3rd of 4ch. 33 mesh patts.

Mesh patt round: 4ch, miss 1ch, * 1tr in tr, 1ch, miss 1ch *, rep from * to *, ending with 1ss in 3rd of 4ch at beg of round. Rep last round 3 more times.

Shape thumb hole:

Next round: 4ch, miss 1ch, (1tr in tr, 1ch, miss 1ch) 9 times, (1tr inserting hook in next tr and in foll 9th tr, leaving 8tr unworked), 1ch, 1tr in same place as last insertion, 1ch, (1tr in tr, 1ch, miss 1ch) 13 times, join with a ss in 3rd of 4ch. 25 mesh patts.
Work mesh patt round 3 times.

Little finger:

1st round: 4ch, miss 1ch, (1tr in tr, 1ch, miss 1ch) 3 times, miss 18tr, (1tr in tr, 1ch, miss 1ch) 3 times, join with a ss in 3rd of 4ch. 7 mesh patts.
Work mesh patt round 5 times.

Last round: 2ch, working in tr of previous round: (tr2tog) 3 times. Fasten off.

Ring finger:

1st round: With palm of glove facing, rejoin yarn to same tr as 3rd tr of 1st round of little finger, 4ch, miss 1ch, (1tr in tr, 1ch, miss 1ch) 3 times, miss 12tr, (1tr in tr, 1ch, miss 1ch) 3 times, 1tr in same tr as 4th tr of 1st round of little finger, 1ch, join with a ss in 3rd of 4ch. 8 mesh patts.
Work mesh patt round 7 times.

Last round: 2ch, (tr2tog) twice, tr3tog. Fasten off.

Middle finger:

1st round: With palm of glove facing, rejoin yarn to same tr as 3rd tr of 1st round of ring finger, 4ch, miss 1ch, (1tr in tr, 1ch, miss 1ch) 3 times, miss 6tr, (1tr in tr, 1ch, miss 1ch) 3 times, 1tr in same tr as 4th tr of 1st round of ring finger, 1ch, join with a ss in 3rd of 4ch. 8 mesh patts.
Work mesh patt round 8 times.

Last round: As given for ring finger.

Forefinger:

1st round: With palm of glove facing, rejoin yarn to same tr as 3rd tr of 1st round of middle finger, 4ch, miss 1ch, (1tr in tr, 1ch, miss 1ch) 6 times, 1tr in same tr as 4th tr of 1st round of middle finger, 1ch, join with a ss in 3rd of 4ch. 8 mesh patts.
Work mesh patt round 7 times.

Last round: As given for ring finger.

Thumb:

1st round: With palm of glove facing, rejoin yarn to same tr as joined tr at inner edge of thumb hole, 4ch, miss 1ch, (1tr in tr, 1ch, miss 1ch) 8 times, join with a ss in 3rd of 4ch. 9 mesh patts.
Work mesh patt round 5 times.

Last round: 2ch, tr2tog, (tr3tog) twice. Fasten off.

Wrist border:

With RS of glove facing, work along lower edge:

1st row: Join yarn to base of last tr of 1st row, 1ch, 1dc in each ch sp and base of each tr all around, turn. 47 sts.

2nd row: 1ch, miss first dc, (1dc in each of 14dc, dc2tog over next 2dc) twice, 1dc in each dc, ending with 1dc in 1ch, turn. 45 sts.

3rd row: 1ch, miss first dc, 1dc in next dc, * (1dc, 3ch, 1ss) in next dc, 1dc in each of 4dc *, rep from * to * 7 more times, (1dc, 3ch, 1ss) in next dc, 1dc in dc, 1dc in 1ch, turn.

4th row: 2ch, miss first dc, 1tr in next dc, * 5ch, miss (1ss, 3ch, 1dc), tr2tog over (next dc and foll 3rd dc) *, rep from * to *, ending with tr2tog over last dc and 1ch, turn.

5th row: 1ch, *9dc in 5ch sp, 1ss in tr2tog *, rep from * to * ending with ss in last tr.
Do not fasten off.

Border to button opening:

1st row: 1ch, work around edge of button opening as foll: 9dc in side edges of rows to inner corner, dc3tog at first inner corner, dc3tog at second inner corner, 10dc in side edges of rows to outer corner, turn.

2nd row: 1ch, miss first dc, 1dc in each of 2dc, 3ch, miss 3dc, 1dc in each st to end. Fasten off.

RIGHT GLOVE:

Work as for Left glove to **. Rejoin yarn to 6th tr of previous round. Complete to match Left glove, reversing shaping by working 13 mesh patts before shaping thumb gusset (and 9 mesh patts after). Start the rounds for fingers with back of glove facing (instead of palm). Work wrist border and border to button opening as given, working buttonhole on opposite edge.

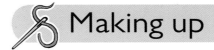

Making up

Thread tails at tops of fingers and thumb through tops of last round of sts, pull up and secure on WS. Use starting tails for fingers and thumb to close gaps between fingers. Sew on buttons to match buttonholes.

Beaded drawstring bag

Select yarn and beads to match your favourite evening outfit and create a unique little bag.

Worked in a lovely silky yarn and rounds of trebles, this pretty bag is enhanced with a beaded pattern and closed with a drawstring. It also has a fabric lining with a firm base to make it more practical.

The Yarn Twilleys Silky (approx. 200m/ 218 yards per 50g/1¾oz ball) is 100% viscose. Perfect for evening projects, it has a slinky feel and elegant sheen. There is a small palette of glamorous pale metallic and rich dark shades.

GETTING STARTED

Working in rounds and working with beads needs some practice.

Size:
Bag is 18cm (7in) high x 9cm (3½in) in diameter

How much yarn:
1 x 50g (1¾oz) ball of Twilleys Silky in Gold (shade 101)

Hook:
3.00mm (UK 11) crochet hook

Additional items:
55g (2oz) of 3mm (⅛in) cube seed beads
Cream sewing thread and needle
36 x 36cm (14 x 14in) piece of cream lining fabric

9cm (3½in) diameter circle of thick card

Tension:
26 sts and 12 rows measure 10cm (4in) square over patt on 3.00mm (UK 11) hook
IT IS ESSENTIAL TO WORK TO THE STATED TENSION TO ACHIEVE SUCCESS

What you have to do:
Thread beads onto yarn before starting work. Work bag base in rounds of trebles. Continue in rounds for sides of bag, working beaded pattern as instructed. At top edge, work eyelet round for drawstrings and finish top with shell edging. Sew and insert lining into bag as instructed. Thread drawstrings through eyelet holes.

Instructions

Abbreviations:

ch = chain(s)
cm = centimetre(s)
patt = pattern
rep = repeat
RS = right side
sps = spaces
ss = slip stitch
st(s) = stitch(es)
tr = treble
WS = wrong side

BAG:

Thread beads onto crochet yarn. With 3.00mm (UK 11) hook make 10ch, join with a ss into first ch to form a ring.

1st round: 3ch (counts as first tr), work 19tr into ring, join with a ss into 3rd of 3ch. 20 sts.

2nd round: 3ch, 1tr into st at base of ch, 2tr into each st to end, join with a ss into 3rd of 3ch. 40 sts.

3rd round: 3ch, 1tr into st at base of ch, 1tr into each of next 3 sts, *2tr into next st, 1tr into each of next 3 sts, rep from * to end, join with a ss into 3rd of 3ch. 50 sts.

4th round: 3ch, 1tr into st at base of ch, 1tr into each of next 4 sts, *2tr into next st, 1tr into each of next 4 sts, rep from * to end, join with a ss into 3rd of 3ch. 60 sts.

5th round: As 4th round. 72 sts.

6th round: 3ch, *slide a bead down to hook, 1ch over bead, miss 1 st, 1tr into next tr, rep from * ending 1ch over bead, miss last st, join with a ss into 3rd of 3ch.

7th–9th rounds: As 6th round.

10th round: 3ch, *1tr into ch above bead, 1tr into next tr, rep from * ending 1tr into ch above bead, join with a ss into 3rd of 3ch.

11th round: 3ch, miss first st, *1tr into next st, rep from * to end, join with a ss into 3rd of 3ch.

12th–23rd rounds: Rep 6th–11th rounds twice.

24th–25th rounds: As 11th round.

26th (eyelet) round: 4ch (counts as first tr and ch sp), miss first 2 sts, *1tr into next st, 1ch, miss next st, rep from * to end, join with a ss into 3rd of 4ch.

27th (edging) round: 3ch, 5tr into st

at base of ch, *miss next ch sp, 1dc into next tr, miss next ch sp, 6tr into next tr, rep from * ending miss next ch sp, 1dc into next tr, miss last ch sp, join with a ss into 3rd of 3ch. Fasten off.

DRAWSTRINGS:

With 3.00mm (UK 11) hook and leaving a long tail of yarn, make 120ch.

1st row: Work 1ss into each ch to end. Fasten off.

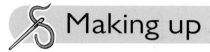

Making up

Make lining:

From lining fabric, cut an 18 x 30cm (7 x 12in) rectangle and two x 12cm (4¾in) diameter circles. With RS facing and raw edges matching, join short edges of rectangle with a narrow double seam. Turn resulting tube RS out and stitch a circle of lining to one end. Press a 1cm (⅜in) turning to WS around open edge of tube. Sew a line of running sts around outer edge of other circle of lining. Place cardboard circle in centre and draw up thread so that card is covered. This will form base of bag.

Assemble bag:

Place lining inside bag and pin the two together so that folded top edge of lining lies just below eyelet round. Slip stitch in place. Place covered card, RS up, at bottom of bag. Secure it with a round of small slip stitches worked from outside of bag, just around edge of crochet base.

Complete drawstrings:

Starting at first shell, thread loose tail of one drawstring through a tapestry needle and weave it through ch sps in eyelet round. Sew two ends of drawstring together, then thread 15 beads onto one loose end. Stitch thread to join to form a loop of beads, then make another two loops in same way. Fasten off ends securely. Starting at opposite side of bag, thread and finish off other drawstring in same way.

Contrast-collar cardigan

Different textures as well as colours make this
a distinctive cardigan.

This classic cardigan has buttons down the front edge and is worked in a fine yarn and pretty lacy pattern. Its neckline is emphasized with a double crochet collar in a striking variegated colourway.

The Yarn

King Cole Merino Blend 4 Ply (approx. 180m/196 yards per 50g/1¾oz ball) is 100% pure new wool. It produces a

fine machine-washable fabric. King Cole Riot DK (approx. 294m/320 yards per 100g/3½oz ball) is 30% wool and 70% acrylic. It is available in several variegated colours.

GETTING STARTED

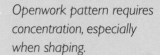 *Openwork pattern requires concentration, especially when shaping.*

Size:
To fit bust: 81– 86[91–97]cm (32–34[36–38]in)
Actual size: 94[110]cm (37[43½]in)
Length: 54[56]cm (21¼[22]in)
Sleeve seam: 46[48]cm (18[19]in)
Note: Figures in square brackets [ ] refer to larger size; where there is only one set of figures, it applies to both sizes

How much yarn:
8[10] x 50g (1¾oz) balls of King Cole Merino Blend 4 ply in colour A – Fuchsia (shade 787)
1 x 100g (3½oz) ball of King Cole Riot DK in colour B – Magic (shade 404)

Hooks:
3.50mm (UK 9) crochet hook
4.00mm (UK 8) crochet hook

Additional items:
6 buttons

Tension:
3 patt reps (3 shells and 3 x 5ch arches) measure 12cm (4¾in) and 16 rows measure 11cm (4¼in) over patt on 3.50mm (UK 9) hook
IT IS ESSENTIAL TO WORK TO THE STATED TENSION TO ACHIEVE SUCCESS

What you have to do:
Work main part of cardigan in 4 ply yarn and lacy openwork pattern with shells. Work fronts and back in one piece up to armholes. Work all edgings in double crochet. Make collar in DK yarn in a variegated colourway and double crochet.

 # Instructions

BACK AND FRONTS: (worked in one piece to armholes)

With 3.50mm (UK 9) hook and A, make 279[327]ch.

1st row: (RS) 2tr into 3rd ch from hook, *miss 2ch, 1dc into next ch, 5ch, miss 5ch, 1dc into next ch, miss 2ch, 5tr – called 1 shell – into next ch, rep from * ending last rep with 3tr into last ch, turn. 22[26] whole shells with a half shell at each end of row.

2nd row: 1ch (does not count as a st), 1dc into st at base of 1ch, *5ch, 1dc into next 5ch arch, 5ch, 1dc into 3rd tr of next 5tr, rep from * ending last rep with 1dc into top of turning ch, turn.

3rd row: *5ch, 1dc into next 5ch arch, 5tr into next dc, 1dc into next 5ch arch, rep from * ending 2ch, 1tr into last dc, turn. 23[27] whole shells.

4th row: 1ch, 1dc into st at base of 1ch, *5ch, 1dc into 3rd

Abbreviations:

beg = beginning
ch = chain(s)
cm = centimetre(s)
cont = continue
dc = double crochet
dc2(3)tog = into each of next 2(3) sts work: (insert hook into st, yrh and draw through a loop), yrh and draw through all 3(4) loops on hook
patt = pattern
rep(s) = repeat(s)
RS = right side
sp = space
ss = slip stitch
st(s) = stitch(es)
tr = treble
WS = wrong side
yrh = yarn round hook

tr of next 5tr, 5ch, 1dc into next 5ch arch, rep from * to end working last dc into 3rd of 5ch, turn.

5th row: 3ch (counts as 1tr), 2tr into st at base of 3ch, *1dc into next 5ch arch, 5ch, 1dc into next 5ch arch, 5tr into next dc, rep from * ending last rep with 3tr into last dc, turn.

The 2nd –5th rows form patt and are repeated throughout. Cont straight in patt until work measures 33cm (13in) from beg, ending with a 2nd patt row.

Divide for fronts and back:
Right front:

Next row: (RS) *5ch, 1dc into next 5ch arch, 5tr into next dc, 1dc into next 5ch arch, rep from * 4[5] times more, 2ch, 1tr into next dc, turn and cont on these sts for Right front. 5[6] whole shells.

Cont straight in patt until armhole measures 12[14]cm (9[2]in) from beg, ending with a 2nd patt row. Fasten off.

Shape neck:

1st row: With RS facing, miss 2 x 5ch arches, rejoin yarn to next dc and patt to end, turn.

2nd row: Patt to last shell, 1dc in 3rd of 5tr, turn.

3rd row: Ss into each of first 3 sts, 1ch, 1dc into next ch, patt to end, turn.

4th row: Patt to last shell, 1dc in 3rd of 5tr, turn.

5th row: As 3rd patt row. 3[4] whole shells.

Cont straight in patt until armhole measures 20[22]cm (4¾[5½]in) from beg, ending

with a WS row. Fasten off.

Back:

With RS facing, miss 2 x 5ch arches, rejoin yarn to next dc, *5ch, 1dc into next 5ch arch, 5tr into next dc, 1dc into next 5ch arch, rep from * 10[12] times, 2ch, 1tr into next dc, turn and cont on these sts for Back. 11[13] whole shells.

Cont straight in patt until Back measures same as Front to shoulder, ending with a WS row. Fasten off.

Left front:

With RS facing, miss 2 x 5ch arches, rejoin yarn to next dc, *5ch, 1dc into next 5ch arch, 5tr into next dc, 1dc into next 5ch arch, rep from * 4[5] times, 2ch, 1tr into last dc, turn and cont on these sts for Left front. 5[6] whole shells. Complete to match Right front, reversing shapings.

SLEEVES: (make 2)

With 3.50mm (UK 9) hook and A, make 87[99]ch.

Work 1st (6[7] whole shells with a half shell at each end of row) to 5th rows as given for Back.

Shape sides:

1st row: 1ch, 2dc into first dc, patt to end, ending 2dc into top of turning ch, turn.

2nd row: 6ch, 1dc into first 5ch arch, patt to end, ending 1dc into last 5ch arch, 3ch, 1tr into last dc, turn.

3rd row: 1ch, 1dc into first tr, 1ch, 1dc into 3ch sp, 5ch, 1dc into 3rd of 5tr, patt to end, ending 1dc into 3rd of 5tr, 5ch, 1dc into 6ch sp, 1ch, 1dc into 3rd of 6ch, turn.

4th row: 3ch, miss st at base of ch, 4tr into next dc, 1dc into next 5ch arch, patt to end, ending 1dc into last 5ch arch, 4tr into next dc, 1tr into last dc, turn.

5th row: 1ch, 1dc into first tr, 2ch, miss 1tr, 1dc into next tr, 5ch, 1dc into first 5ch arch, patt to end, ending 1dc into last 5ch arch, 5ch, miss 2tr, 1dc into next tr, 2ch, 1dc into top of turning ch, turn.

6th row: 8ch, 1dc into first 5ch arch, patt to end, ending 1dc into last 5ch arch, 5ch, 1tr into last dc, turn.

7th row: 1ch, 1dc into first tr, 3ch, 1dc into first 5ch arch, patt to end, ending 1dc into

8ch sp, 3ch, 1dc into 3rd of 8ch, turn.

8th row: 1ch, 2dc into first dc, 5tr into next dc, patt to end, ending 1dc into last 5ch arch, 5tr into next dc, 2dc into last dc, turn.

9th row: 1ch, 1dc into first dc, 4ch, 1dc into 3rd of 5ch, patt to end, ending 1dc into 3rd of 5ch, 4ch, 1dc into last dc, turn.

10th row: 4ch, 1dc into 4ch sp, 5ch, 1dc into next 5ch arch, patt to end, ending 1dc into last 5ch arch, 5ch, 1dc into 4ch sp, 1ch, 1tr into last dc, turn.

11th row: 1ch, 1dc into first tr, 5ch, 1dc into next 5ch arch, patt to end, ending 5ch, 1dc into 3rd of 4ch, turn.

12th – 14th rows: As 3rd to 5th patt rows of Back and fronts. 7[8] whole shells with a half shell at each end of row. Rep 1st to 14th rows twice more. 9[10] whole shells with a half shell at each end of row.

Cont straight in patt until Sleeve measures 47[49]cm (18½[19¼]in) from beg, ending with a WS row. Fasten off.

COLLAR:

With 4.00mm (UK 8) hook and B, make 83ch.

1st row: (WS) 1dc into 3rd ch from hook, 1dc into each ch to end, turn. 82 sts.

2nd row: 1ch (counts as 1dc), miss st at base of ch, 1dc into each st to end, 1dc into turning ch, turn.

Rep last row 12 times more.

Shape collar:

Next row: 1ch, miss st at base of ch, dc2tog, 1dc into each dc to last 3 sts, dc2tog, 1dc into turning ch, turn.

Next row: As 2nd row.

Rep last 2 rows twice more. 76 sts.

Next row: 1ch, miss st at base of ch, dc3tog, 1dc into each

st to last 4 sts, dc3tog, 1dc into turning ch, turn.

Rep last row twice more. 64 sts. Fasten off.

With RS facing, rejoin B to lower right-hand corner and work 1 row of dc evenly up first short end, across top and down other short end. Fasten off.

BUTTON BAND:

With 3.50mm (UK 9) hook and RS facing, rejoin A to corner of neck on Left front, 1ch, work in dc evenly down left front edge, turn.

Next row: 1ch (counts as 1dc), miss st at base of ch, 1dc in each dc to end, working last dc in 1ch, turn. Rep last row 4 times more. Fasten off. Mark positions of 6 buttons, the first to come 1cm (⅜in) up from lower edge, the last 1cm (⅜in) down from neck edge, with the others spaced evenly between.

BUTTONHOLE BAND:

With 3.50mm (UK 9) hook and RS facing, rejoin A to corner of lower edge on Right front, 1ch, work in dc evenly up right front edge, turn. Work 1 row in dc as given for Button band.

1st buttonhole row: (RS) 1ch, 1dc into each dc making buttonholes to correspond with markers on Left front by working 2ch, miss 2dc.

2nd buttonhole row: Work in dc, working 2dc into each 2ch sp on previous row.

Work 2 rows more in dc. Fasten off.

LOWER EDGING:

With 3.50mm (UK 9) hook and RS facing, rejoin A to lower corner of Button band, 1ch, work in dc evenly along lower edge, turn.

Work 2 rows in dc as given for Button band. Fasten off.

CUFFS:

With 3.50mm (UK 9) hook and RS facing, rejoin A to lower edge of Sleeve, 1ch, work in dc evenly along lower edge, turn. Work 2 rows in dc as given for Button band. Fasten off.

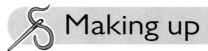

Making up

Join shoulder seams. Sew first row of collar to neck edge, beg at centre of buttonhole band and ending at centre of button band. Sew sleeves into armholes, sewing top 2cm (¾in) of side edges to underarm sts on Back and fronts. Join sleeve seams. Sew on buttons.

Mesh curtain

A great project for a beginner, this cotton curtain is quick to make and easy to hang.

Let soft light in with this cotton curtain worked in a filet mesh pattern. Gently gathered, the curtain is suspended from a pole inserted through the hanging loops at the top.

GETTING STARTED

Even though working in pattern from a chart, this is just a straight piece of fabric.

Size:
Curtain measures 70cm (27½in) wide x 61cm (24in) deep, not including hanging loops

How much yarn:
4 x 100g (3½oz) balls of Patons 100% Cotton DK in White (shade 02691)

Hook:
3.50mm (UK 9) crochet hook

Tension:
1 patt rep (16 sts) measures 7cm (2¾in) wide and 1 patt rep (8 rows) measures 7.5cm (3in) deep on 3.50mm (UK 9) hook
IT IS ESSENTIAL TO WORK TO THE STATED TENSION TO ACHIEVE SUCCESS

What you have to do:
Work main fabric in filet pattern, following a chart for blocks and spaces. Add borders afterwards in double crochet. Work hanging loops into top edge border.

The Yarn
Patons 100% Cotton DK (approx. 210m/229 yards per 100g/3½oz ball) is a pure cotton yarn with a slight twist, which enhances the appearance of the crochet stitches. It can be machine washed and there are plenty of shades.

Instructions

Abbreviations:

ch = chain(s)
cm = centimetre(s)
cont = continue
dc = double crochet
foll = follows
patt = pattern
rep = repeat
RS = right side
sp(s) = space(s)
ss = slip stitch
st(s) = stitch(es)
tr = treble(s)
WS = wrong side

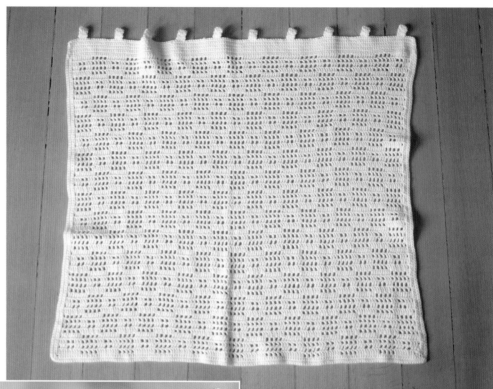

CURTAIN:

With 3.50mm (UK 9) hook make 157ch.

1st row: (WS) 1tr into 4th ch from hook, reading 1st row of chart from right to left, work as foll: *1tr into each of next 8ch (4 blocks), (1ch, miss 1ch, 1tr into next ch) 4 times (4 sps), rep from * to last 9ch, 1tr into each of next 8ch (4 blocks), 1tr into last ch (edge st), turn.

2nd row: 3ch (counts as first tr), 1tr into next tr, reading 2nd row of chart from left to right, work as foll: *1tr into each of next 2tr (1 block), (1ch, miss 1tr, 1tr into next tr) twice (2 sps), 1tr into each of next 2tr (1 block), (1ch, miss 1ch, 1tr into next tr) 4 times (4 sps), rep from * to last 9 sts, 1tr into each of next 2tr (1 block), (1ch, miss 1tr, 1tr into next tr) twice (2 sps), 1tr into each of next 2tr (1 block), 1tr into 3rd of 3ch (edge st), turn.

3rd row: 3ch, miss first tr, 1tr into next tr, reading 3rd row of chart from right to left, cont as foll: *1tr into each of next 2tr (1 block), (1ch, miss 1ch, 1tr into next tr) twice (2 sps), 1tr into each of next 2tr (1 block), (1ch, miss 1ch, 1tr into next tr) 4 times (4 sps), rep from * to last 9 sts, 1tr into each of next 2tr (1 block), (1ch, miss 1ch, 1tr into next tr) twice (2 sps), 1tr into each of next 2tr (1 block), 1tr into 3rd of 3ch, turn.

Cont in patt from chart until 8 rows have been completed. Rep these 8 rows until

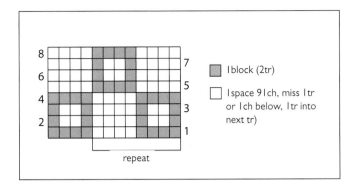

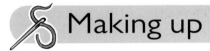

I block (2tr)

I space (I ch, miss I tr or I ch below, I tr into next tr)

repeat

work measures 56cm (22in) from beg, ending with a 4th or 8th patt row. Fasten off.

Sides and lower border:

1st row: With 3.50mm (UK 9) hook and RS of work facing, join yarn to top left-hand corner, I ch, 2dc into side edge of each row to corner, I dc, I ch and I dc into same place at corner, work I dc into base of each ch along lower edge, I dc, I ch and I dc into same place at corner, cont in dc up side edge to top right corner, turn. 159 sts.

2nd row: I ch, miss first dc, I dc into each dc and I dc, I ch and I dc into ch sp at each corner, ending with ss into first ch. Fasten off.

Top border:

1st row: With 3.50mm (UK 9) hook and RS of work facing, join yarn to side edge of 2nd row or border at top right-hand corner of curtain, I ch, I dc into side edge of next border row, I dc into each st along top edge, I dc into side edge of each of 2 border rows. 159 sts.

2nd row: I ch, miss first dc, I dc into each dc, working last dc into I ch, turn. Rep last row until top border measures 3cm (1¼in), ending with a WS row.

Hanging loop row: I ch, miss first dc, I dc into each of next 8dc, turn, *I ch (counts as first dc), miss first dc, I dc into each of next 3dc, turn **, rep from * to ** until loop fits easily around pole, fasten off; rejoin yarn to top of last dc worked into top edge, I dc into each of next 16dc, turn ***, rep from * to *** ending last rep with I dc into each of last 5dc, I dc into I ch, do not fasten off.

Final row: Cont in dc down side edge of curtain, working 2dc into side edge of every 3 rows of top border, then I dc into each dc and I dc, I ch and I dc into ch sp at each corner, ending at top right corner. Fasten off.

Making up

Press carefully or block as specified on yarn label. Fold each hanging loop in half to WS and use yarn tails to sew firmly in place.

Beaded zip clutch

Fill this neat little bag with life's essentials and then you're ready for a night out.

This pretty bag is worked in an openwork pattern incorporating beads. It is lined in a toning fabric and has a zipped opening.

GETTING STARTED

★★ *Beading requires practice and some sewing skills needed for a good finish.*

Size:
Bag measures 25cm (10in) wide x 15cm (6in) deep

How much yarn:
2 x 50g (1¾oz) balls of Rowan Cotton Glacé in Blood Orange (shade 445)

Hook:
3.00mm (UK 11) hook

Additional items:
88 x 5mm (¼in) amber glass beads
Matching sewing thread and fine needle
Tapestry needle, 25cm (10in) nylon zip
Two 26 x 15cm (10¼ x 6in) rectangles of tangerine cotton fabric for lining

Tension:
3 patt repeats and eight rows measure 7cm (2¾in) square over patt on 3.00mm (UK 11) hook
IT IS ESSENTIAL TO WORK TO THE STATED TENSION TO ACHIEVE SUCCESS

What you have to do:
Thread beads onto one ball of yarn before starting work. Work front in openwork pattern, including beaded stitches. Work back in same pattern but omitting beads. Sew fabric lining with zipped opening.

The Yarn
Rowan Cotton Glacé (approx. 115m/125 yards per 50g/1¾oz ball) is 100% mercerised cotton. Its weight is between 4-ply and double knitting and it is machine-washable. There is a good colour range to team with your choice of beads.

Instructions

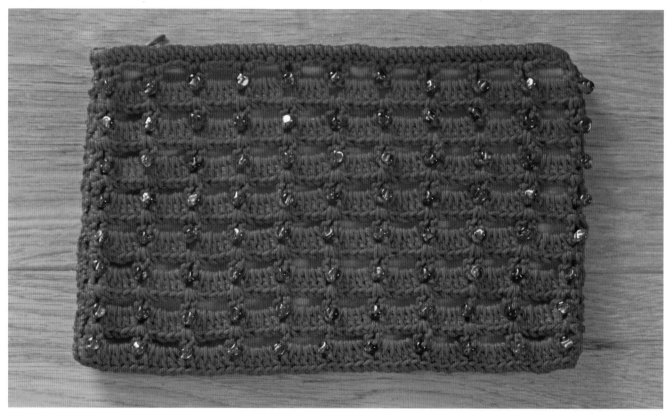

Abbreviations:
ch = chain(s)
cm = centimetre(s)
gr(s) = groups(s)
htr = half treble
patt = pattern
rep = repeat
RS = right side
sp = space
ss = slip stitch
st(s) = stitch(es)
tr = treble
WS = wrong side

THREADING BEADS

Before you start work, thread the beads on to one ball of yarn. To do this, thread a sewing needle with a 30cm (12in) length of sewing cotton and knot the ends together. Slide the thread through the eye of the needle so that the knot lies halfway down one side of the loop. Pass the end 20cm (8in) of one ball of the crochet yarn through the loop. Now thread the beads on to the needle, one at a time. Slide each one along the sewing thread loop, over the loose end of crochet yarn and down on to the ball of yarn.

BAG FRONT:

With 3.00mm (UK 11) hook make 55ch using yarn threaded with beads.
Foundation row: (RS) 1htr into 3rd ch from hook, 1htr into each ch to end, turn. 54 sts.
1st row: 3ch (counts as first tr), miss st at base of ch, *1tr into next st, then slide a bead

down yarn so that it sits on top of st, work 1ss pulling yarn so that bead lies securely at back of work – called bead 1, 1tr into next st, 3ch, miss next 3 sts, rep from * to last 3 sts, bead 1 into next st, 1tr into next st, 1tr into 2nd of 2ch, turn.

2nd row: 3ch, miss st at base of ch, 1tr into each of next 2tr, *5tr into next 3ch sp, rep from * to last 3 sts, 1tr into each of next 2tr, 1tr into 3rd of 3ch, turn.

3rd row: 3ch, miss st at base of ch, bead 1 into next st, miss next tr, 1tr into sp between missed tr and first 5tr gr, *3ch, miss 5tr gr, bead 1 into next sp between grs, 1tr into same sp, rep from * ending bead 1 into sp after last 5tr gr and next tr, miss 1tr, 1tr into next tr, 1tr into 3rd of 3ch, turn. The 2nd and 3rd rows form patt. Rep them 6 times more, then work 2nd row again. Fasten off.

BAG BACK:
Work as given for Front but omit beads.

Making up

Place front and back together with WS facing. Turn upside down so that foundation rows form top edge, then join remaining three sides.

Press a 1cm (⅜ in) turning to WS along one long edge of each lining rectangle. With RS facing, sew folded edge of each lining rectangle to each side of zip. Start each stitch line at top end of zip and allow bottom end to project over fabric.

Open zip. With RS facing, pin remaining three sides of lining together and machine stitch 1cm (⅜ in) in from edge. Trim seam allowance to 6mm (¼ in) and neaten with a zigzag stitch.

Place lining inside bag and pin in place so that seam between zip and lining lies along top of foundation rows. Slip stitch neatly in place along this line with matching sewing thread.

Twenties flower hat

This close-fitting hat is designed with the glamorous style of the 1920s in mind.

A pretty shell pattern is worked in the round to make this snug-fitting hat. The self-coloured 'floral' decorations are created from strips of double crochet.

The Yarn Patons 100% Cotton 4 Ply (approx. 330m/ 360 yards per 100g/3½oz ball) is a 100% cotton machine-washable yarn with a slight sheen, ideal for filet crochet. There are plenty of colours.

GETTING STARTED

 Working in rounds may take some practice.

Size:
To fit an average-sized adult head

How much yarn:
1 x 100g (3½oz) ball of Patons 100% Cotton 4-ply in Nougat (shade 2715)

Hooks:
3.50mm (UK 9) crochet hook
4.00mm (UK 8) crochet hook

Tension:
18 sts and 22 rows measure 10cm (4in) square over dc on 4.00mm (UK 8) hook
IT IS ESSENTIAL TO WORK TO THE STATED TENSION TO ACHIEVE SUCCESS

What you have to do:
Work crown in rounds of double crochet, increasing as directed. Continue in rounds of openwork shell pattern. Make strips of double crochet, then roll them up and stitch to create 'flowers'.

Instructions

Abbreviations:

beg = beginning
ch = chain(s)
cm = centimetre(s)
cont = continue
dc = double crochet
foll = follows
patt = pattern
rep = repeat
sp = space
ss = slip stitch
st(s) = stitch(es)
tr = treble

HAT:

With 4.00mm (UK 8) hook make 5ch, join with a ss into first ch to form a ring.

1st round: 1ch (counts as first dc), 7dc into ring, join with a ss into first ch. 8dc.

2nd round: 1ch, 1dc into st at base of ch, 2dc into each dc to end, join with a ss into first ch. 16dc.

3rd round: 1ch, 1dc into st at base of ch, 1dc into next dc, *2dc into next dc, 1dc into next dc, rep from * to end, join with a ss into first ch. 24dc.

4th round: 1ch, 1dc into st at base of ch, 1dc into each of next 2dc, *2dc into next dc, 1dc into each of next 2dc, rep from * to end, join with a ss into first ch. 32dc.

5th round: 1ch, 1dc into st at base of ch, 1dc into each of next 3dc, *2dc into next dc, 1dc into each of next 3dc, rep from * to end, join with a ss into first ch. 40dc.

6th round: 1ch, 1dc into st at base of ch, 1dc into each of next 4dc, *2dc into next dc, 1dc into each of next 4dc, rep from * to end, join with a ss into first ch. 48dc.

7th round: 1ch, 1dc into each dc to end, join with a ss into first ch.

8th round: 1ch, 1dc into st at base of ch, 1dc into each of next 5dc, *2dc into next dc, 1dc into each of next 5dc, rep from * to end, join with a ss into first ch. 56dc.

9th round: 1ch, 1dc into st at base of ch, 1dc into each of next 6dc, *2dc into next dc, 1dc into each of next 6dc, rep from * to end, join with a ss into first ch. 64dc.

10th round: 1ch, 1dc into st at base of ch, 1dc into each of next 7dc, *2dc into next dc, 1dc into each of next 7dc, rep from * to end, join with a ss into first ch. 72dc.

11th round: As 7th round.

12th round: 1ch, 1dc into st at base of ch, 1dc into each of next 11dc, *2dc into next dc, 1dc into each of next 11dc, rep from * to end, join with a ss into first ch. 78dc.

13th round: As 7th round.

Cont in patt as foll:

Foundation round: 4ch, miss first 3 sts, *1dc into next dc, 3ch, miss next 2dc, rep from * to end, join with a ss into 1st of 4ch.

1st round: Ss into first 3ch sp, 3ch (counts as 1tr), 4tr (first shell) in same 3ch sp, *5tr into next 3ch sp (shell made), rep from * to end, join with a ss into 3rd of 3ch.

2nd round: Ss to centre tr on first shell, 4ch (counts as 1dc and 3ch), *1dc into centre tr on next shell, 3ch, rep from * to end, join with ss into 1st of 4ch.

3rd round: Ss to centre ch of first 3ch sp, 1dc, 3ch, *1dc into next 3ch sp, 3ch, rep from * to end, join with a ss into first dc.

The last 3 rounds form patt. Rep them 3 times more, then work 1st round again.

Next round: Ss to centre tr on first shell, 3ch (counts as 1dc and 2ch), *1dc into centre tr on next shell, 2ch, rep from * to end, join with a ss into first of 3ch.

Change to 3.50mm (UK 9) hook.

Next round: 1ch (counts as 1dc), *2dc in next 2ch sp, 1dc in next dc, rep from * ending 2dc into last 2ch sp, join with a ss into first ch, turn.

Next round: 1ch, 1dc in each dc to end, join with a ss into first ch, turn.

Rep last round twice more. Fasten off.

LARGE FLOWER:

With 4.00mm (UK 8) hook make 41ch.

Next row: 1dc into 2nd ch from hook, 1dc into each ch to end, turn. 40 sts.

Next row: 1ch (counts as first dc), miss st at base of ch, 1dc into each dc to end, turn.

Work 1 row in dc.

Next row: Make 30ch, 1dc into 3rd ch from hook, 1dc into each ch and dc to end, turn. 69 sts.

Next row: 1ch, miss st at base of ch, *1dc into each of next 2dc, 2dc into next dc, rep from * ending with 1dc into next dc, 1dc in turning ch, turn. 91 sts.

Work 1 more row in dc. Fasten off.

SMALL FLOWER: (make 2)

With 4.00mm (UK 8) hook make 31ch.

Next row: 1dc into 2nd ch from hook, 1dc into each ch to end, turn. 30 sts.

Next row: 1ch (counts as first dc), miss st at base of ch, 1dc into each dc to end, turn.

Work 1 row in dc.

Next row: Make 22 ch, 1dc into 3rd ch from hook, 1dc into each ch and dc to end, turn. 51 sts.

Next row: 1ch, miss st at base of ch, *1dc into each of next 2dc, 2dc in next dc, rep from * ending with 1dc into next dc, 1dc into turning ch, turn. 67 sts.

Work 1 more row in dc. Fasten off.

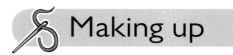

Making up

For flowers, beg at narrowest end (inside of flower) and, winding around to form a coil, sew base ch edge as you go along. Sew to side of hat as shown in picture.

Trio of cushions

Large and small granny squares make a coordinating
set of beautiful cushions.

Based on a palette of the pretty colours found in a field of wildflowers, this mix 'n' match set of cushions combines two over-size granny squares in complementary colours with a third that is a patchwork of smaller squares.

GETTING STARTED

★ *Once under way, it is easy to keep the pattern correct on these large squares.*

Size:
Cushions measure 40cm (16in) square

How much yarn:
1 x 50g (1¾oz) ball of Sirdar Click DK in colours
A – Verve (shade 110) and 2 balls in
D – Pistachio (shade 117)
2 x 100g (3½oz) balls of Sirdar Country Style DK in each of colours B – Rosehip (shade 527) and
C – Sweet Cicely Pink (shade 587)
1 x 50g (1¾oz) ball of Sirdar Escape DK in colour
E – Temptation (shade 194)

Hook:
4.00mm (UK 8) crochet hook

Additional items:
3 x 40cm (16in) square cushions with plain covers
Note: Colour of cushion shows through gaps in crochet; we used light beige cushions

Tension:
First 4 rounds of patt measure 10cm (4in) square worked on 4.00mm (UK 8) hook
IT IS ESSENTIAL TO WORK TO THE STATED TENSION TO ACHIEVE SUCCESS

What you have to do:
Make two cushions with back and front worked separately in rounds of treble clusters with three-chain spaces at corners. Vary colours for each cushion as instructed. Make one cushion with patchwork front, incorporating sixteen small squares all with final round worked in same colour. Crochet back and front together.

The Yarn
These use Sirdar yarns: Click DK (approx. 150m/164 yards per 50g/ 1¾oz ball) is 70% acrylic and 30% wool in solid and variegated shades; Country Style DK (approx. 318m/347 yards per 100g/3½oz ball) has 45% acrylic, 40% nylon and 15% wool and Escape DK (approx. 110m/120 yards per 50g/1¾oz ball) is 51% wool and 49% acrylic.

Instructions

Abbreviations:

ch = chain
cm = centimetre(s)
cont = continue
dc = double crochet
foll = follows
inc = increasing
rep = repeat
sp = space
ss = slip stitch
st(s) = stitch(es)
tr = treble
WS = wrong side

CUSHION 1
Front:

With 4.00mm (UK 8) hook and A, make 5ch, join with a ss in first ch to form a ring.

1st round: With A, 3ch (counts as first tr), 2tr in ring, 3ch, (3tr in ring, 3ch) 3 times, join with a ss in 3rd of 3ch. Fasten off A.

2nd round: Join B to any 3ch sp, 3ch, 2tr in same sp, (3tr, 3ch, 3tr in next ch sp) 3 times, 3tr in first ch sp, 3ch, join with a ss to 3rd of 3ch. Fasten off B.

3rd round: Join C to any 3ch sp, 3ch, 2tr in same sp, *3tr in sp between clusters, (3tr, 3ch, 3tr) in next 3ch sp, rep from * twice more, 3tr in sp between clusters, 3tr in first ch sp, 3ch, join with a ss in 3rd of 3ch. Fasten off C.

4th round: Join D to any 3ch sp, 3ch, 2tr in same sp, *(3tr in sp between clusters) twice, (3tr, 3ch, 3tr) in next 3ch sp, rep from * twice more, (3tr in sp between clusters) twice, 3tr in first ch sp, 3ch, join with a ss in 3rd of 3ch. Fasten off D.

5th round: Join E to any 3ch sp, 3ch, 2tr in same sp, *(3tr in sp between clusters) 3 times, (3tr, 3ch, 3tr) in next 3ch sp, rep from * twice more, (3tr in sp between clusters) 3 times, 3tr in first ch sp, 3ch, join with a ss in 3rd of 3ch. Fasten off E.

Using each colour in turn, cont in this way, inc 1 more cluster on each side on every

round, until 18 rounds in all have been completed, ending with a round in colour C.

Back:
Work 18 rounds as given for Front, working in colours as foll:
1 round each A, B, C, D and C; 11 rounds B and 2 rounds C.

CUSHION 2
Front:
Work as given for Front of Cushion 1 but working in colours as foll: (1 round each A, B, C, D, C, B, A, E) twice; 1 round each A and B.
Back:
With B only, work 18 rounds as given for Front.

CUSHION 3
Front:
Basic square:
Work as given for 1st–4th rounds of Cushion 1. Make 16 squares in total, varying colours in 1st–3rd rounds and always working 4th round in colour D.
Back:
Work 18 rounds as given for Front of Cushion 1, working in colours as foll: 15 rounds in C and 3 rounds in B.

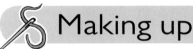 Making up

CUSHION 1
With WS facing, pin front and back together around three sides, matching corners carefully. With back of cushion facing, join C to back at first pinned corner, insert 4.00mm (UK 8) hook through loops at top of first tr then through corresponding loops on front and work 1dc, cont to join three sides in this way, working 1dc in corresponding pairs of sts and 3dc into ch sp at each corner. Insert cushion, pin fourth sides together and join them in dc.

CUSHION 2
With B instead of C, work as given for Cushion 1.

CUSHION 3
Arrange squares in four rows of four and, using D, sew together vertically and then horizontally in rows to form front. Using C, crochet together as given for Cushion 1, noting that 1dc should be worked in ch sp at either side of joins between squares.

Cutaway shrug

Styled with a nod to the 1950s, this neat shrug creates a striking silhouette.

Worked in a firm but soft fabric, this shrug curves at the front edges and has a small collar. It is made in two pieces from the sleeves to the centre back and front edges.

GETTING STARTED

★★★ *Unusual construction and plenty of shaping make this challenging even for confident crocheters.*

Size:
To fit bust: 76–81[86–91:97–102]cm
(30–32[34–36:38–40]in)
Actual width across back: 43[48:53]cm (17[19:21]in)
Length from shoulder: 31[33.5:35.5]cm
(12¼[13¼:14]in)
Sleeve seam: 32cm (12½in)
Note: *Figures in square brackets [ ] refer to larger sizes; where there is only one set of figures, it applies to all sizes*

How much yarn:
8[9:10] x 50g (1¾oz) balls of Sublime Cashmere Merino Silk DK in Miss Scarlet (shade 167)

Hook:
4.00mm (UK 8) crochet hook

Tension:
17 sts and 12 rows measure 10cm (4in) square over patt on 4.00mm (UK 8) hook
IT IS ESSENTIAL TO WORK TO THE STATED TENSION TO ACHIEVE SUCCESS

What you have to do:
Start at cuff edge of sleeve and work sleeve first, then add extra stitches for front and back. Finish each section at centre front. Work in pattern comprising pairs of treble stitches. Shape front curve as directed. Work double crochet collar directly onto neckline edge.

The Yarn
Sublime Cashmere Merino Silk DK (approx. 116m/126 yards per 50g/1¾oz ball) contains 75% extra fine merino wool, 20% silk and 5% cashmere. This luxurious blend produces fabrics that are firm and yet soft. There is a large palette of subtle and strong shades.

 Instructions

Abbreviations:
beg = beginning; **ch** = chain; **cm** = centimetre(s)
cont = continue; **dc** = double crochet
dec = decreased; **foll** = follows; **inc** = increased
patt = pattern(s); **rem** = remain; **rep** = repeat

RS = right side; **sp** = space; **ss** = slip stitch;
st(s) = stitch(es); **tog** = together; **tr** = treble;
tr2(3)tog = work 2(3) tr as specified leaving last loop of each on hook, yrh and draw through all 3(4) loops;
WS = wrong side; **yrh** = yarn round hook

Note: Sleeve, Back and Front are worked in one piece to centre of back and front.

LEFT SIDE:
Sleeve:
With 4.00mm (UK 8) hook make 41[45:49]ch.

Foundation row: (RS) 2tr into 5th ch from hook, *miss 1ch, 2tr into next ch (pair of tr worked), rep from * to last 2ch, miss 1ch, 1tr into last ch, turn. 38[42:46] sts; 18[20:22] pairs of tr plus 1 st at each end.

Patt row: 3ch (counts as 1tr), miss tr at base of ch, *2tr into sp at centre of next pair of tr, rep from * to end, 1tr into top of 3ch, turn. This row forms patt and is repeated throughout. Patt 2 rows more.

Sleeve shaping:
1st row: (RS) 3ch, 1tr into st at base of ch (1 st inc), *2tr into sp at centre of next pair of tr, rep from * to end, 2tr into 3rd of 3ch (1 st inc), turn.

2nd row: 3ch, 1tr into next tr, *2tr into sp at centre of next pair of tr, rep from * to last 2 sts, 1tr into next tr, 1tr into 3rd of 3ch, turn.

3rd–5th rows: As 2nd row.

6th row: 3ch, 2tr into sp between first and 2nd tr (1 st inc), *2tr into sp at centre of next pair of tr, rep from * ending 2tr into sp between last 2 sts (1 st inc), 1tr into 3rd of 3ch, turn.

7th–10th rows: As patt row.

Work 1st to 10th rows twice more. 50[54:58] sts; 24[26:28] pairs of tr plus 1 st at each end. Cont straight in patt until work measures 32cm from beg, ending with a WS row.

Left back and front:
With 4.00mm (UK 8) hook and a separate ball of yarn, make 28[30:32]ch for Left front (when working Right side these sts will be for the Back). Fasten off and leave on one side. Return to Sleeve and with 4.00mm (UK 8) hook, make 30[32:34]ch for Back (when working Right side these sts will be for the Right front).

Next row: 2tr into 5th ch from hook, *miss 1ch, 2tr into next ch (pair of tr worked), rep from * 11[12:13] times more, miss last ch.

With RS facing, work 2tr into first tr of Sleeve, patt across 48[52:56] sts of Sleeve, 2tr into top of 3ch, then patt across length of 28[30:32]ch as foll: **miss 1ch, 2tr into next ch, rep from ** 12[13:14] times more, miss 1ch, 1tr into last ch, turn. 106[114:122] sts; 52[56:60] pairs of tr plus 1tr at each end of row. Patt 1 row. ***

Shape front curve:
1st row: (RS) 3ch, patt to last pair of tr, tr2tog into sp at centre of last pair of tr (1 st dec), 1tr into 3rd of 3ch, turn.

2nd row: 3ch, tr2tog working 1st leg into tr2tog of last row and 2nd leg into sp at centre of next pair of tr (1 st dec), 1tr into same sp, patt to end, turn. Rep last 2 rows 6[7:8] times more. 92[98:104] sts; 45[48:51] pairs of tr plus 1 st at each end.

Next row: 3ch, patt to last two pairs of tr, 1tr into sp at centre of next pair of tr, tr3tog working 1st leg into same sp as last tr, then 2nd and 3rd legs into sp at centre of last pair of tr (1 pair of tr dec), 1tr into 3rd of 3ch, turn.

Next row: 3ch, tr3tog working 1st and 2nd legs into sp at centre of first pair of tr then 3rd leg into sp at centre of next pair of tr (1 pair of tr dec), 1tr into same sp, patt to end, turn. 88[94:100] sts; 43[46:49] pairs of tr plus 1 st at each end.

Back:
Next row: 3ch, patt next 50[54:58] sts, 1tr into sp at centre of next pair of tr, turn and work on these 52[56:60] sts for Back.

Patt a further 7[8:9] rows. Fasten off.

RIGHT SIDE:

Work as given for Left side to ***.

Shape front curve:

1st row: (RS) 3ch, tr2tog into sp at centre of first pair of tr (1st dec), patt to end, turn.

2nd row: Patt to last 4 sts, 1tr into sp at centre of last pair of tr, tr2tog working 1st leg into same sp as last tr and 2nd leg into tr2tog of last row (1st dec), 1tr into 3rd of 3ch, turn.

Rep last 2 rows 6[7:8] times more. 92[98:104] sts; 45[48:51] pairs of tr plus 1 st at each end.

Next row: 3ch, tr3tog working 1st and 2nd legs into sp at centre of first pair of tr, then 3rd leg into sp at centre of next pair of tr (1 pair of tr dec), 1tr into same sp, patt to end, turn.

Next row: 3ch, patt to last two pairs of tr, 1tr into sp at centre of next pair of tr, tr3tog working 1st leg into same sp as last tr, then 2nd and 3rd legs into sp at centre of last pair of tr (1 pair of tr dec), 1tr into 3rd of 3ch, turn. 88[94:100] sts; 43[46:49] pairs of tr plus 1 st at each end. Fasten off.

Back:

With RS facing and counting from edge of back, rejoin

yarn at centre of 26th[28th:30th] pair of tr, 3ch, (2tr into sp at centre of next pair of tr) 25[27:29] times, 1tr into 3rd of 3ch, turn. Cont on these 52[56:60] sts for Back. Patt a further 7[8:9] rows.

COLLAR:

With RS facing, join back seam with a row of ss. Fasten off.

With 4.00mm (UK 8) hook and RS facing, rejoin yarn to last st on last row worked for Right front curve.

Shape for collar:

1st row: (RS) 3ch, tr3tog working 1st and 2nd legs into sp at centre of first pair of tr, then 3rd leg into sp at centre of next pair of tr (1 pair of tr dec), 1tr into same sp*, (2tr into sp at centre of next pair of tr on Right front) 16[17:18] times, work 1 pair of tr into end of each of 16[18:20] rows across back, (2tr into sp at centre of next pair of tr on Left front) 16[17:18] times, **1tr into sp at centre of next pair of tr, tr3tog working 1st leg into same sp as last tr, then 2nd and 3rd legs into sp at centre of last pair of tr (1 pair of tr dec), 1tr into 3rd of 3ch, turn.

2nd row: Work as 1st row to *, patt to last two pairs of tr, work as 1st row from ** to end.

Rep last row 6[7:8] times more. Fasten off.

 ## Making up

Join side and sleeve seams.

Edging:

With 4.00mm (UK 8) hook and RS facing, rejoin yarn to Left side seam, 1ch (counts as 1dc), work in dc evenly along Back and around Front edges, join with a ss into 1ch at beg of round, do not turn.

Next round: 1dc back into last st just worked, *1dc into next st to right, rep from * to end, join with a ss into first dc. Fasten off.

Cuffs:

With 4.00mm (UK 8) hook and RS facing, rejoin yarn at Sleeve seam, 1ch (counts as 1dc), work in dc evenly around cuff edge, join with a ss into 1ch at beg of round, do not turn.

Next round: 1dc back into last st just worked, *1dc into next st to right, rep from * to end, join with a ss into first dc. Fasten off.

Lavender sachets

Scented sachets make the perfect home-made gift and are a creative way of using your lavender stems.

This pair of lavender bag and purse are both worked from the same lacy pattern in traditional crochet cotton, then filled with a coloured fabric sachet containing dried lavender, and trimmed with organza bows.

The Yarn

Twilleys Lyscordet (approx. 200m/218 yards per 50g/1¾oz ball) is 100% mercerised cotton. It is a traditional crochet cotton with a slight twist, which produces good stitch definition. It comes in white as well as plenty of colours.

 GETTING STARTED

Bag and purse are constructed from straight strips of fabric.

Size:
Bag: 16.5 x 13cm (6½ x 5in)
Purse: 11 x 13cm (4½ x 5in)

How much yarn:
1 x 50g (1¾oz) ball of Twilleys Lyscordet in White (shade 78) for both sachets

Hook:
2.50mm (UK 12) crochet hook

Additional items:
Dried lavender and 24 x 13cm (9½ x 5in) rectangle of sheer fabric (such as organza) for each sachet
Needle and matching sewing thread
1.3m (1⅜ yards) 25mm (1in) wide organza ribbon

Tension:
10 sps and 18 rows measure 10cm (4in) square on 2.50mm (UK 12) hook
IT IS ESSENTIAL TO WORK TO THE STATED TENSION TO ACHIEVE SUCCESS

What you have to do:
For bag and purse, work straight strip of fabric in lacy pattern with clusters and chain arches. For bag, work shell edging around top edge. For purse, make up into an envelope shape and work shell edging along flap. Sew fabric into sachet and fill with dried lavender. Trim bag and purse with organza ribbon bows.

Instructions

Abbreviations:

beg = beginning
ch = chain
cm = centimetre(s)
cont = continue
dc = double crochet
foll = follows
patt = pattern
rep = repeat
RS = right side
sp(s) = space(s)
ss = slip stitch
st(s) = stitch(es)
tog = together
tr = treble
WS = wrong side
yrh = yarn round hook

LAVENDER BAG:

**With 2.50mm (UK 12) hook make 43ch.

Foundation row: (RS) 1dc into 7th ch from hook, *3ch, miss next 2ch, 1dc into next ch, rep from * to end, turn. 13 sps.

Next row: 3ch, leaving loop of each on hook work 3tr all into next sp, yrh and draw through all 4 loops on hook (cluster formed), *3ch, 1dc into next sp, 3ch, 1 cluster into next sp, rep from * ending with 1tr into 4th of 6ch, turn. 7 clusters.

Cont in patt as foll:

1st row: 4ch, 1dc into next sp, *3ch, 1dc into next sp, rep from * ending with 3ch, 1dc into 3rd of 3ch, turn.

2nd row: 3ch, 1dc into first sp, *3ch, 1 cluster into next sp, 3ch, 1dc into next sp, rep from * ending with 1tr into 3rd of 4ch, turn. 6 clusters.

3rd row: 4ch, 1dc into next sp, *3ch, 1dc into next sp, rep from * ending with 3ch, 1dc into 3rd of 3ch, turn. 13 sps.

4th row: 3ch, 1 cluster into next sp, *3ch, 1dc into next sp, 3ch, 1 cluster into next sp, rep from * ending with 1tr into 4th of 4ch, turn. 7 clusters.

These 4 rows form patt. Cont in patt until work measures 31cm (12¼in) from beg, ending with a 1st patt row. Fasten off.**

LAVENDER PURSE:

Work as given for Lavender bag from ** to **.

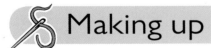 ## Making up

LAVENDER BAG:

Block to size. Fold crochet in half widthways, with WS tog, and join side seams.

Edging:

With 2.50mm (UK 12) hook and RS facing, join yarn to one side seam and work (2dc into next sp, 3dc into each of next 12 sps around top edge) twice, join with a ss into first dc. 76dc.

Shell round: 1dc into first dc, *miss next dc, 4tr all into next dc, miss next dc, 1dc into next dc, rep from * to end, join with a ss into first dc. Fasten off.

Lavender sachet:

With RS facing, fold fabric in half to measure 13 x 12cm (5 x 4¾in). Taking 1cm (⅜in) seam allowance, join seams, leaving an opening for filling. Trim seams and snip corners. Turn sachet to RS. Fill with dried lavender and slip stitch opening closed. Insert sachet into bag. Cut 75cm (30in) of ribbon and tie in a bow around bag; trim ribbon ends to desired length.

LAVENDER PURSE:

Block to size. Fold 11cm (4¼in) below top edge on to RS, matching patt rows. Join side seams.

Edging:

With 2.50mm (UK 12) hook and WS of work facing, join yarn to first sp of flap, 1ch, 2dc into first sp, 3dc into each sp to within last sp, 2dc into last sp, turn. 37dc.

Shell row: 1dc into first dc, *miss next dc, 3tr all into next dc, miss next dc, 1dc into next dc, rep from * to end. Fasten off.

Lavender sachet:

Work as given for Lavender bag sachet. Insert sachet into purse. Fold flap over and secure with a few stitches in the centre; do not cut thread. Tie remaining ribbon in a bow and sew onto flap.

Retro cushion

Make this over-sized cushion in a palette of vintage colours to create a fabulous retro accessory.

The front of this large cushion is a patchwork of small squares each with a circular design at the centre and rotating the same four colours throughout. The same colours are used in treble stripes on the back.

GETTING STARTED

★ ★ *Making individual squares and working cushion back are easy but attention to detail is needed for a good finish.*

Size:
To fit 55cm (22in) square cushion pad

How much yarn:
3 x 50g (1¾oz) balls of Debbie Bliss Rialto Aran in each of four colours – Green (shade 10), Rust (shade 33), Duck-egg Blue (shade 23) and Charcoal (shade 26)

Hook:
5.00mm (UK 6) crochet hook

Additional item:
55cm (22in) square cushion pad

Tension:
Each square motif measures 13cm (5in); 16 sts and 10 rows measure 10cm (4in) square over tr on 5.00mm (UK 6) hook
IT IS ESSENTIAL TO WORK TO THE STATED TENSION TO ACHIEVE SUCCESS

What you have to do:
Using four colours, make 16 square motifs in rounds as described. Sew squares together to form one large square for cushion front. Work an edging around cushion front. Make cushion back in rows of trebles and two-row stripes of each colour. Crochet cushion front and back together.

The Yarn
Debbie Bliss Rialto Aran (approx. 80m/ 87 yards per 50g/1¾oz ball) contains 100% merino wool. It produces a soft fabric with good stitch definition that can be machine washed at a low temperature. There is a fantastic range of retro shades.

Instructions

Abbreviations:

beg = beginning
ch = chain(s)
cm = centimetre(s)
cont = continue
dc = double crochet
dtr = double treble
patt = pattern
rep = repeat
RS = right side
sp = space
ss = slip stitch
st(s) = stitch(es)
tog = together
tr = treble
WS = wrong side

FRONT:
Square motif:
With 5.00mm (UK 6) hook and 1st colour, make 6ch, join with a ss into first ch to form a ring.

1st round: With 1st colour, 3ch (counts as first tr), work 11tr into ring changing to 2nd colour on last part of last st, join with a ss into 3rd of 3ch. 12 sts.

2nd round: With 2nd colour, 3ch, 1tr into same place as ss, 2tr into each st to end, changing to 3rd colour on last part of last st and joining with a ss into 3rd of 3ch. 24 sts.

3rd round: With 3rd colour, 3ch, 1tr into same place as ss, 1tr into next st, *2tr into next st, 1tr into next st, rep from * to end, changing to 4th colour on last part of last st and joining with a ss into 3rd of 3ch. 36 sts.

4th round: With 4th colour, 3ch, 1tr into same place as ss, 1tr into each of next 2 sts, *2tr into next st, 1tr into each of next 2 sts, rep from * to end, changing to 1st colour on last part of last st and joining with a ss into 3rd of 3ch. 48 sts.

5th round: With 1st colour, 3ch, into same place as ss work (1tr, 1dtr, 2tr) for corner, 1tr into each of next 2 sts, 1dc into each of next 7 sts, 1tr into each of next 2 sts, *into next st work (2tr, 1dtr, 2tr) for corner, 1tr into each of next 2 sts, 1dc into each of next 7 sts, 1tr into each

of next 2 sts, rep from * twice more, join with a ss into 3rd of 3ch.

6th round: With 1st colour, 3ch, miss st at base of ch, 1tr into next st, into next st (centre st of previous corner) work (2tr, 1dtr, 2tr), *1tr into each st to centre st of next corner, into next st work (2tr, 1dtr, 2tr), rep from * twice more, 1tr into each st to end, join with a ss into 3rd of 3ch. Fasten off.

Make 16 motifs in total (we made 4 in each of 4 colourways, rotating the positions of the 4 colours).

Lay motifs out on a flat surface, RS up, in any order that you like (or use our photograph as a guide to positioning colours) to make one large square with 4 motifs in each of 4 rows. Beg at top right-hand corner and working in horizontal rows, sew each motif to the next with yarn that matches one square, working into back loop only of pairs of corresponding sts. When all 4 horizontal rows have been joined, sew vertical rows tog in same way.

Edging:

With 5.00mm (UK 6) hook and RS facing, join 1st colour to side edge of large square, 2ch (counts as first tr), miss st at base of ch, then work 1tr into each tr (do not work into dtr at each side of joins) and 1tr into each join of smaller squares all around, working (1tr, 1dtr and 1tr) into each dtr at corner, changing to 2nd colour on last part of last st and joining with a ss into 2nd of 2ch. 81 sts in each side between corner dtr.

With 2nd colour, work another round in tr in same way but in each corner dtr work (2tr, 1dtr, 1tr). Fasten off.

BACK:

Note: 2ch only is used to count as first tr in patt rows. With 5.00mm (UK 6) hook and 1st colour, make 87ch.

Foundation row: (RS) 1tr into 3rd ch from hook, 1tr into each ch to end, turn. 86 sts.

Patt row: 2ch (counts as first tr), miss st at base of ch, 1tr into each st to end, working last tr into 2nd of 2ch, turn. Rep last row throughout, working 2 rows in each of 4 colours in turn, until work measures 54cm (21¼cm) from beg, ending with a WS row. Fasten off.

Making up

Press lightly according to directions on ball band.

With 5.00mm (UK 6) hook, WS of Front and Back together, RS of Front facing and working into both pieces, join 3rd colour to centre dtr at lower right-hand corner and work 1ch, 2dc into same dtr, 1dc into each tr of Front and row-ends of Back to centre dtr at next corner, 3dc into centre dtr, cont to join Front and Back in this way along two more sides. Insert cushion pad and cont to join last side, join with a ss into first ch. Fasten off.

Beaded purse

A simple design showcases your favourite beads
or charms worked along the top edge of the bag.

This dainty purse is designed with a long strap so that it can be worn across the body. The simple textured fabric is decorated around the top edge with beads and charms that are worked into the fabric.

GETTING STARTED

★ ★ *There is no shaping but working in rounds and adding in beads requires some practice.*

Size:
Finished bag measures 13.5cm (5¼in) wide x 16cm (6¼in) high

How much yarn:
1 x 100g (3½oz) ball of Patons 100% Cotton DK in Orchard (shade 721)

Hook:
3.00mm (UK 11) crochet hook

Additional items:
1.2m (1¼ yards) of 15mm (⅝in) wide Petersham ribbon in matching colour
Sewing needle and matching thread
32 white beads
16 plastic leaf-shaped charms with single hole

Tension:
23 sts and 24 rows measure 10cm (4in) square over patt on 3.00mm (UK 11) hook
IT IS ESSENTIAL TO WORK TO THE STATED TENSION TO ACHIEVE SUCCESS

What you have to do:
Make bag in one piece, starting at base and working in rounds. Thread beads and charms on to yarn and work them into pattern around top edge. Sew Petersham ribbon to back of strap to prevent it stretching. Sew ends of strap to inside of bag.

The Yarn
Patons 100% Cotton DK (approx. 210m/229 yards per 100g/3½oz ball) is a lustrous mercerized cotton yarn, perfect for craft projects. It is machine washable and available in a wide range of great colours.

Instructions

Abbreviations:

ch = chain
cm = centimetre(s)
cont = continue
dc = double crochet
foll = follows
htr = half treble
patt = pattern
rep = repeat
RS = right side
ss = slip stitch
st(s) = stitch(es)
tr = treble
WS = wrong side
yrh = yarn round hook

PURSE:

With 3.00mm (UK 11) hook make 31ch.

Foundation round: 1dc into 2nd ch from hook, 1dc into each ch to last ch, 3dc into last ch, do not turn but cont along other side of foundation ch as foll: 1dc into each of next 29ch, 3dc into next ch, join with a ss into first dc. 64 sts.

1st round: 1ch (does not count as a st), 1dc into first st, *insert hook into same st as last dc just worked, yrh and draw through a loop, (insert hook into next st, yrh and draw through a loop) twice, yrh and draw through all 4 loops – called 1 cluster, 1ch, rep from * to last st, 1dc into last st, join with ss into back loop of first dc.

2nd round: Miss first dc, ss into first cluster, 1ch, 1dc into first cluster, 1dc into each ch and each cluster, ending 1dc into last dc, 1dc into missed dc, ss into both loops of first dc.

The last 2 rounds form patt. Rep them 13 times more.

29th round: 2ch (counts as first htr), miss st at base of ch, 1htr into back loop only of each st to end, join with a ss into 2nd of 2ch.

30th–32nd rounds: 1ch (does not count as a st), 1dc in each st to end, join with a ss into first dc. Fasten off. Thread 32 white beads, then 16 charms on to ball of yarn. With WS facing, rejoin yarn to last st worked and cont as foll:

33rd round: 1ch (does not count as a st), then with WS facing and working in opposite direction to previous rounds, work 1dc into first st, 1dc into each of next 2 sts, slide a single charm down yarn until it sits snugly against RS of work and, keeping charm in position, work 1dc into next st, *1dc into each of next 3 sts, slide charm down yarn so it sits against RS of work, 1dc into next st, rep from * to end, join with a ss into first dc.

34th round: As 30th–32nd rounds.

35th round: 1ch, 1dc into first st, *slide a single bead down yarn so that it sits against RS of work, 1dc into each of next 2 sts, rep from * to last st, slide a bead down yarn so that it sits against RS of work, 1dc into last st, join with a ss into first dc. Fasten off.

STRAP:

With 3.00mm (UK 11) hook make 3ch, 1tr into 3rd ch from hook, turn, *yrh, miss top of tr and the 2 strands to left of tr and insert hook from right to left through single strand at left edge, yrh and draw loop through, (yrh and draw through 2 loops on hook) twice, turn. Rep from * until strap measures 110cm (43in) (or length required). Fasten off.

Making up

Sew Petersham ribbon to one side of strap, folding under 1cm (³⁄₈in) of ribbon at each end to neaten. Sew ends of strap securely to sides of bag, positioning them inside bag and 1cm (³⁄₈in) below top edge.

Nordic sweater

Follow the trend for Scandi style with this colourful jumper.

Worked in traditional colours, this sweater has an all-over textured pattern and rib-effect borders with Scandinavian-style motifs on a circular yoke.

GETTING STARTED

★ ★ ★ *With its texture and circular patterned yoke, this design will challenge a competent crocheter.*

Size:

To fit bust: 81–86[91–97]cm (32–34[36–38]in)
Actual size: 95[102]cm (37½[40]in)
Length at centre back: 61[65]cm (37½[40]in)
Sleeve seam: 43.5[45]cm (24[25½]in)
Note: Figures in square brackets [ ] refer to larger size; where there is only one set of figures, it applies to both sizes

How much yarn:

15[17] x 50g (1¾oz) balls of King Cole Merino Blend DK in colour A – Cranberry (shade 703)
1 ball in each of two other colours: B – Asparagus (shade 785) and C – White (shade 1)

Hooks:

3.50mm (UK 9) crochet hook
4.00mm (UK 8) crochet hook

Tension:

17 sts and 13.5 rows measure 10cm (4in) square over raised st patt on 4.00mm (UK 8) hook
IT IS ESSENTIAL TO WORK TO THE STATED TENSION TO ACHIEVE SUCCESS

What you have to do:

Work back, front and sleeves first up to armhole shaping in main colour and raised stitch pattern. Work circular yoke in rows over all four sections, shaping as instructed and joining into rounds at end to work neckband in rib pattern. Use two contrast colours with main colour to work pattern on yoke. Add rib patterned cuffs and border to complete garment.

The Yarn

King Cole Merino Blend DK (approx. 112m/122 yards per 50g/1¾oz ball) contains 100% pure new wool in a machine-washable format. It produces an attractive fabric and there is a wide range of colours to choose from.

 Instructions

BACK:
With 4.00mm (UK 8) hook and A, make 82[88]ch.
Foundation row: (WS) 1htr in 3rd ch from hook, 1htr in each ch to end, turn. 81[87] sts.
Cont in raised st patt as foll:
1st row: (RS) 2ch (counts as first htr), miss st at base of ch, *1rtrf in next htr, 1htr in each of next 5htr, rep from * to last 2 sts, 1rtrf in next htr, 1htr in 2nd of 2ch, turn.
2nd row: 2ch, miss st at base of ch, 1htr in each st to end, working last htr in 2nd of 2ch, turn.
3rd row: 2ch, miss st at base of ch, 1htr in each of next 3htr, *1rtrf in next htr, 1htr in each of next 5htr, rep from * to last 5 sts, 1rtrf in next htr, 1htr in each of next 3htr, 1htr in 2nd of 2ch, turn.
4th row: As 2nd.
These 4 rows form patt. Rep them 11[12] more times, ending with a 4th patt row. 49[53] rows in all. **
Shape armholes:
*** **1st row:** Ss in each of first 6 sts, 2ch, miss st at base of ch, htr2tog over next 2htr, patt as set to last 8 sts, htr2tog over next 2htr, 1htr into next htr, turn leaving 5 sts unworked.
2nd row: 2ch, miss st at base of ch, htr2tog over next 2 sts, patt as set to last 3 sts, htr2tog over next 2 sts, 1htr in 2nd of 2ch, turn.

Abbreviations:

alt = alternate
ch = chain(s)
cm = centimetre(s)
cont = continue
dc = double crochet
dec = decreasing
foll = follow(s)(ing)
htr = half treble
htr2tog = (yrh, insert hook as directed, yrh and draw a loop through) twice, yrh and draw through all 5 loops on hook
inc = increase(d)
patt = pattern
rep = repeat
RS = right side
rtrb = raised tr back: inserting hook from right to left and from back to front, work 1tr around stem of next st
rtrf = raised tr front: inserting hook from right to left and from front to back, work 1tr around stem of next st
ss = slip stitch
st(s) = stitch(es)
tr = treble
tr2tog = (yrh and insert hook as indicated, yrh and draw a loop through, yrh and draw through 2 loops on hook) twice, yrh and draw through all 3 loops on hook
WS = wrong side
yrh = yarn round hook

Keeping patt correct, rep last row twice more. *** 63[69] sts. Fasten off.

FRONT:
Work as given for Back to **.
Shape front neck and armhole:
First side: 1st row: Ss in each of first 6 sts, 2ch, miss st at base of ch, htr2tog over next 2htr, patt 19 sts as set, htr2tog over next 2 sts, 1htr in next st, turn. 23 sts.
2nd row: Ss in each of first 9 sts, 2ch, miss st at base of ch, htr2tog over next 2 sts, patt 9 sts, htr2tog over next 2 sts, 1htr in 2nd of 2ch, turn. 13 sts.
3rd row: 2ch, miss st at base of ch, htr2tog over next 2 sts, 1rtrf in next st as set, htr2tog over next 2 sts, 1htr in next st, turn leaving 6 sts unworked. 5 sts.
4th row: Ss in each of first 3 sts, 2ch, miss st at base of ch, htr2tog over next st and 2nd of 2ch. Fasten off.
Second side: With RS of work facing, miss 21[27] sts at centre front and rejoin yarn in next st.
1st row: 2ch, miss st at base of ch, htr2tog over next 2 sts, patt 19 sts as set to last 8 sts, htr2tog over next 2 sts, 1htr in next st, turn leaving 5 sts unworked. 23 sts.
2nd row: 2ch, miss st at base of ch, htr2tog over next 2 sts, patt 9 sts, htr2tog over next 2 sts, 1htr in next st, turn leaving 8 sts unworked. 13 sts.

3rd row: Ss in each of first 7 sts, 2ch, miss st at base of ch, htr2tog over next 2 sts, 1rtrf in next st as set, htr2tog over next 2 sts, 1htr in 2nd of 2ch, turn. 5 sts.
4th row: 2ch, miss st at base of ch, htr2tog over next 2 sts leaving 2 sts unworked. Fasten off.

SLEEVES: (make 2)
With 4.00mm (UK 8) hook and A, make 46[52]ch. Work foundation row as given for Back. 45[51] sts. Beg 1st[3rd] patt row, work 6[8] rows in raised st patt, ending with a 2nd patt row. 7[9] rows in all.
Shape sleeve:
Inc row: 2ch, miss st at base of ch, 2htr in next htr, patt as set to last 2 sts, 2htr in next st, 1htr in 2nd of 2ch, turn. 1 st inc at each end of row. Work 5 rows straight, working extra sts into patt. Rep last 6 rows 6 more times, then work inc row again. 61[67] sts. Work 3 rows straight, then work inc row again. 63[69] sts. Work 1 row straight, ending with a WS row. 55[57] rows in all.
Shape sleeve top:
Work as given for Back armhole shaping from *** to ***. 45[51] sts. Fasten off.

YOKE:
Note: When working yoke patt, always change colour on last part of last st in old colour. Lay old colour across top of sts and

enclose it as you work sts in new colour until you need to change colour again. Change colour as before, gently pulling on enclosed yarn so it lies flat, but not too tight.

Join Sleeves to Front at both armholes. Join left Sleeve to Back, so leaving right back armhole seam open.

With 4.00mm (UK 8) hook and RS facing, join A to top right corner of back.

1st yoke row: 1ch (counts as first dc), miss st at base of ch, work 59[62]dc evenly across top of Back, dec 3[6] times evenly to end with last of these dc in armhole seam (60[63] sts across back); dec evenly work 40[42]dc across top of Left sleeve; 1dc in seam; 58[61]dc evenly across top of Front; 1dc in seam; 41[43]dc evenly across top of Right sleeve, turn. 201[211] sts.

2nd yoke row: 2ch, miss st at base of ch, 1htr in each dc to end, work last htr in 1ch and changing to B, turn.

3rd yoke row: 2ch in B, miss st at base of ch, cont in htr: 1 B, *2 A, 3 B, rep from * to last 4 sts, 2 A, 2 B, turn. Fasten off B.

4th yoke row: With A, 2ch, miss st at base of ch, 1htr in each htr to end, working last htr in 2nd of 2ch, turn.

5th yoke row: 2ch in A, changing to C, *2 C, 5 A, 2 C, 1 A, rep from * to end, turn.

6th yoke row: 2ch in A, changing to C, *3 C, 3 A, 3 C, 1 A, rep from * to end, turn.

7th yoke row: 2ch in A, changing to C, *4 C, 1 A, rep from * to end, changing to B, turn. Fasten off C.

8th yoke row: 2ch in B, *9 A, 1 B, rep from * to end, turn. Fasten off B.

9th yoke row: As 7th yoke row, but do not fasten off C.

10th yoke row: As 6th yoke row.

11th yoke row: As 5th yoke row. Fasten off C.

12th yoke row: As 4th yoke row, changing to B at end.

13th yoke row: As 3rd yoke row.

Cont in A throughout.

14th yoke row: 2ch, miss st at base of ch, 1htr in each of next 3htr, *htr2tog over next and foll alt st, 1htr in each of next 7htr, rep from * to last 7 sts, htr2tog over next and foll alt st, 1htr in each of next 3htr, 1htr in 2nd of 2ch, turn. 161[169] sts.

15th yoke row: 2ch, miss st at base of ch, 1htr in each st, ending 1htr in 2nd of 2ch, turn.

Rep last row 2[4] more times.

Next row: 2ch, miss st at base of ch, 1htr in each of next 2htr, *htr2tog over next and foll alt st, 1htr in each of next 5htr, rep from * to last 6 sts, htr2tog over next and foll alt st, 1htr in each of next 2htr, 1htr in 2nd of 2ch, turn. 121[127] sts. Work 2 more rows straight in htr. 20[22] yoke rows in all.

Neckband:

Change to 3.50mm (UK 9) hook.

1st size only:

1st round: (RS) 3ch, miss st at base of ch, *1rtrf in next htr, tr2tog over next 2htr, 1rtrf in next htr, 1tr in next htr, rep from * to last 5 sts, 1rtrf in next htr, tr2tog as set, 1rtrf in next htr, join with 1tr in 2nd of 2ch tog with ss under 3ch at beg of round. 96 sts. (First 3ch and last ss count as 1 st.)

2nd size only:

1st round: (RS) 3ch, miss st at base of ch, *1rtrf in next htr, tr2tog over next 2htr, 1rtrf in next htr, 1tr in next htr, rep from * to last st, 1rtrf in 2nd of 2ch, join with ss under 3ch at beg of round. 102 sts. (First 3ch and last ss count as 1 st.)

Both sizes:

Rib round: 2ch, miss st at base of ch, *1rtrf in next rtrf, 1rtrb in next st, rep from * to last st, 1rtrf in next rtrf, join with a ss under 2ch. Rep last round once more. Fasten off.

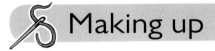 # Making up

Join side and sleeve seams. Join right back armhole and yoke seam.

Cuffs:

With 3.50mm (UK 9) hook and RS of work facing, join A to base of sleeve seam and work in base of sts in foundation ch as foll:

1st round: 2ch, miss st at base of ch, 1htr in each of next 3[0] sts, *htr2tog over next 2 sts, 1htr in each of next 3 sts, rep from * to last 2[1] sts, 1htr in last 2[1] sts, join with a ss under 2ch at beg of round. (First 2ch and last ss count as 1 st.) 38[42] sts.

2nd round: 2ch, miss st at base of ch, *1rtrf in next st, 1rtrb in foll st, rep from * to last st, 1rtrf in last st, join with a ss under 2ch.

Rep last round twice more. Fasten off.

Lower border:

With 3.50mm (UK 9) hook and RS of work facing, join A to base of one side seam and work in base of sts in foundation ch as foll:

1st round: 2ch, miss st at base of ch, 1htr in each st, join with a ss under 2ch at beg of round, making an even number of sts in all. (First 2ch and last ss count as 1 st.)

2nd round: As 2nd round of cuff.

Rep last round until border measures 6.5cm (2½in). Fasten off.

Press carefully according to directions on ball band.

Lacy table runner

Give a classic crochet favourite a contemporary twist
with elegant, yet simple, square motifs.

Worked in natural-coloured cotton yarn and a lacy, openwork pattern, this runner with a picot edging is an updated version of a traditional classic for the table.

GETTING STARTED

Easy introduction to lace patterns as this one is simple to keep correct.

Size:
Runner is 28cm (11in) wide x 76cm (30in) long

How much yarn:
2 x 100g (3½oz) balls of DMC Petra No. 3 in beige (shade 5712)

Hook:
3.50mm (UK 9) crochet hook

Tension:
1 patt repeat measures 6cm (2⅜in) square over patt on 3.50mm (UK 9) hook
IT IS ESSENTIAL TO WORK TO THE STATED TENSION TO ACHIEVE SUCCESS

What you have to do:
Make foundation chain and work foundation row of trebles separated by chain spaces. Continue in pattern with lacy blocks separated by chain spaces. Work double crochet edging with picots around outer edge.

The Yarn
DMC Petra No. 3 (approx. 280m/305 yards per 100g/3½oz ball) is a soft and supple 100% mercerized cotton thread that is perfect for crochet. It can be machine washed and there are plenty of colours to choose from.

 Instructions

RUNNER:
With 3.50mm (UK 9) hook make 80ch.
Foundation row: (RS) 1tr into 8th ch from hook, *2ch, miss 2ch, 1tr into next ch, rep from * to end, turn. 25 ch sps.
1st row: 5ch (counts as first tr and 2ch), miss tr at base of ch, 1tr into next tr, *4ch, 1dtr into each of next 4tr, 4ch, 1tr into next tr, 2ch, 1tr into next tr, rep from * to end, working last tr into 3rd of turning ch, turn.
2nd row: 5ch, miss tr at base of ch, 1tr into next tr, *4ch, 1dc into each of next 4dtr, 4ch, 1tr into next tr, 2ch, 1tr into next tr, rep from * to end, working last tr into 3rd of 5ch, turn.
3rd row: 5ch, miss tr at base of ch, 1tr into next tr, *4ch, 1dc into each of next 4dc, 4ch, 1tr into next tr, 2ch, 1tr

Abbreviations:
ch = chain(s)
cm = centimetre(s)
cont = continue
dc = double crochet
dtr = double treble
foll = follows
patt = pattern
rep = repeat
RS = right side
sps = spaces
ss = slip stitch
tr = treble

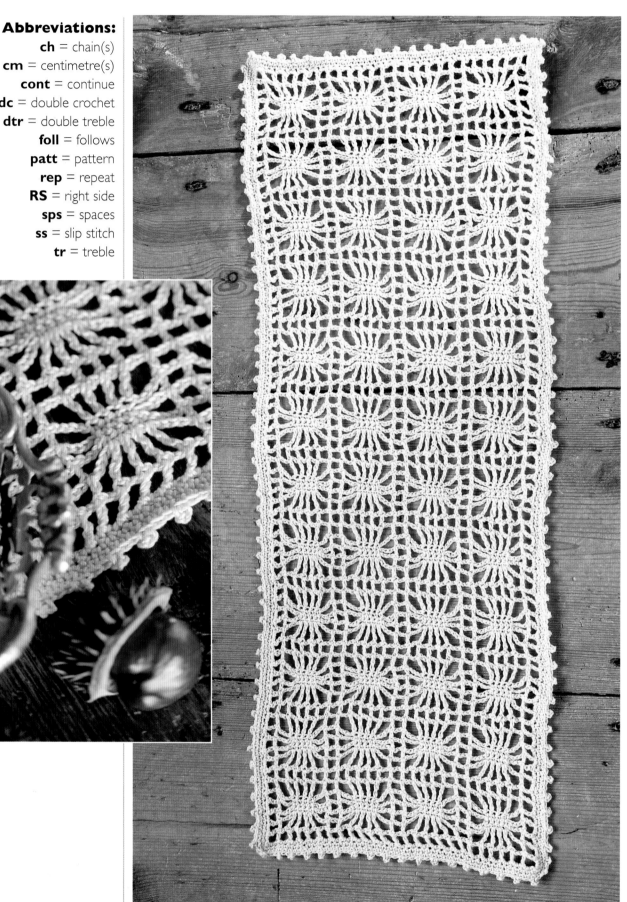

into next tr, rep from *, working last tr into 3rd of 5ch, turn.

4th row: As 3rd row.

5th row: 5ch, miss tr at base of ch, 1tr into next tr, *2ch, (1dtr into next dc, 2ch) 4 times, 1tr into next tr, 2ch, 1tr into next tr, rep from * to end, working last tr into 3rd of 5ch, turn.

6th row: 5ch, miss tr at base of ch, 1tr into next tr, *2ch, (1tr into next dtr, 2ch) 4 times, 1tr into next tr, 2ch, 1tr into next tr, rep from * to end, working last tr into 3rd of 5ch, turn. 25 ch sps.

The 1st–6th rows form patt. Rep them 11 times more. Do not fasten off, but cont as foll:

Edging:

Next round: Work in dc around entire outer edge, working 2dc into each space and 3dc into each corner st, join with a ss into first dc.

Next round: 1dc into each dc and 3dc into centre dc at each corner all round, join with a ss into first dc.

Next round: *1dc into each of next 3dc, 3ch, ss into last dc worked, rep from * all round, join with a ss into first dc.

Press lightly under a damp cloth with a warm iron to set patt.

Square-motif scarf

Start with one square and then keep adding until you have a pretty wraparound scarf.

Made from pretty openwork squares joined together with rows of trebles, this long narrow scarf has an edging of plain trebles and the short ends are trimmed with knotted tassels.

The Yarn
DMC Petra No. 3 (approx. 280m/305 yards per 100g/3½oz ball) is a mercerized thread in 100% cotton. It produces a soft, supple machine-washable fabric with a silky sheen. There is a good colour range.

GETTING STARTED

Pattern gets easier once you have practised with first square but careful making up is required for a neat finish.

Size:
12cm (4¾in) wide x 138cm (54in) long, excluding fringes

How much yarn:
1 x 100g (3½oz) ball of DMC Petra No. 3 in Pale Blue (shade 5800)

Hook:
3.00mm (UK 11) crochet hook

Tension:
Motif measures 10cm (4in) square worked on

3.00mm (UK 11) hook
IT IS ESSENTIAL TO WORK TO THE STATED TENSION TO ACHIEVE SUCCESS

What you have to do:
Make first square in rounds of openwork pattern finished with a round of trebles, then add two rows of trebles onto two opposite sides of square. Make subsequent squares in same way, join each square to previous one along treble rows using slip stitch. Work treble edging around completed scarf, making chain spaces in short ends for tassels. Make fringe by knotting tassels through both short ends.

Instructions

Abbreviations:

beg = beginning
ch = chain(s)
cm = centimetre(s)
cont = continue
dc = double crochet
foll = follows
rep = repeat
RS = right side
sp = space
ss = slip stitch
st(s) = stitch(es)
tog = together
tr = treble
tr2(3)tog = into arch, work (yrh, insert hook into arch, yrh and draw through a loop, yrh and draw through 2 loops on hook) 2(3) times, yrh and draw through all 3(4) loops on hook
WS = wrong side
yrh = yarn round hook

SCARF:
First motif:

With 3.00mm (UK 11) hook make 6ch, join with a ss into first ch to form a ring.

1st round: 1ch (does not count as a st), (1dc into ring, 15ch) 12 times, join with a ss into first dc.

2nd round: Ss into each ch to centre of first 15ch arch, 3ch, tr2tog into same arch (counts as first tr3tog – called cluster), *4ch, tr3tog into same arch, (4ch, 1dc into next arch) twice, 4ch, tr3tog into next arch, rep from * 3 times more, omitting tr3tog at end of last rep, join with a ss into top of first cluster.

3rd round: Ss into next arch, 3ch, tr2tog into same arch, *4ch, tr3tog into same arch, (4ch, 1dc into next arch, 4ch, tr3tog into next arch) twice, rep from * 3 times more, omitting tr3tog at end of last rep, join with a ss into top of first cluster.

4th round: Ss into next arch, 3ch (counts as first tr), 4tr into same arch, *(1tr into top of next cluster, 3tr into next arch, 1tr into next dc, 3tr into next arch) twice, 1tr into top of next cluster, 5tr into next arch, rep from * 3 times more, omitting 5tr at end of last rep, join with a ss into 3rd of 3ch, ss into each of next 2tr and turn work.

Next row: 3ch, miss st at base of ch, 1tr into each of next 22 sts, turn. **
Rep last row once more.

Fasten off.

Turn motif through 180 degrees so that opposite edge of square is at top edge. With WS facing, join yarn to centre tr of 5tr at top right-hand corner, 3ch, miss st at base of ch, 1tr into each of next 22 sts, turn. ***

Work 1 more row in tr on these 23 sts.

Fasten off.

Second motif:

Work as given for First motif to ***.

Join motifs:

Place first (previous) motif on top of second (just worked) motif with RS facing and matching end with extra rows (note that motif with yarn attached is at back) and work joining row as foll:

3ch, ss into first st on First motif, *1tr into next st on Second motif, ss into corresponding st on First motif, rep from * to end, working last ss into 3rd of 3ch. Fasten off. Cont in this way, joining each motif just worked to previous motif, until there are 8 motifs joined together.

End motif: (make 2)

Work as given for First motif to **, then join one to 8th motif and other to first motif.

Edging:

With 3.00mm (UK 11) hook and RS of work facing, join yarn about halfway along one long edge of scarf, 3ch (counts as first tr), miss st at base of ch, *work 1tr into each tr along squares and (2tr into first and 3tr into 2nd row end) twice across joining rows to 3rd of 5tr at corner of first short end, 1tr into 3rd of 5tr, (1ch, miss 1tr, 1tr into each of next 3tr) 5 times across short end, 1ch, miss 1tr, 1tr into 3rd of 5tr*, rep from * to * along other long edge and short end of scarf, then cont in tr until beg of round is reached, join with a ss into 3rd of 3ch. Fasten off.

Fringe:

Cut 5 x 36cm (14in) lengths of yarn for each tassel. Fold strands in half. Insert crochet hook from back to front through first ch sp at one end of scarf, and pull folded strands through from front to back to form a loop. Pull cut end of strands through loop and draw loop up gently to knot tassel in place. Rep in each ch sp along both ends of scarf. Trim fringes level.

Target pouffe

Inject a pop of colour into your décor with this bold
and beautiful ottoman.

This striking pouffe is worked completely in the round in a chunky yarn. It has multi-coloured, target-style stripes on the top and base, with the sides in a bright solid colour.

The Yarn

King Cole Aero Chunky (approx. 78m/85 yards per 100g/3½oz ball) is a practical mixture of 80% premium acrylic and 20% wool. This hard-wearing yarn with a distinctive twist can be machine washed and is available in a wide range colours.

GETTING STARTED

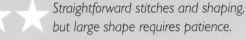 *Straightforward stitches and shaping, but large shape requires patience.*

Size:

Approximately 48cm (19in) in diameter x 24cm (9½in) high

How much yarn:

3 x 100g (3½oz) balls of King Cole Aero Chunky in colour A – Strawberry (shade 447)
1 ball in each of five colours: B – Petrol (shade 435); C – Melon (shade 445); D – Fern (shade 449); E – Plum (shade 444) and F – Tomato (shade 434)

Hook:

10.00mm (UK 000) crochet hook

Additional item:

15 litres (½ cubic foot) polystyrene ball beanbag filling in stockinette bag

Tension:

First 3 rounds measure 16cm (6¼in) in diameter on 10.00mm (UK 000) hook
IT IS ESSENTIAL TO WORK TO THE STATED TENSION TO ACHIEVE SUCCESS

What you have to do:

Starting at centre of pouffe top, work throughout in rounds of trebles, shaping as directed. Work stripes as directed, always changing to new colour on last part of last stitch in old colour. Insert bag of filling before working final rounds to enclose it.

Instructions

Abbreviations:

ch = chain(s)

cm = centimetre(s)

cont = continue

foll = following

ss = slip stitch

st(s) = stitch(es)

tr = treble

tr2tog = (yrh, insert hook into next st, yrh and draw a loop through, yrh and draw through first 2 loops on hook) twice, yrh and draw through all 3 loops on hook

yrh = yarn round hook

Note: If you have difficulty completing the pouffe with filling inside, place it on a table and sit close to it, rotating the work as you go.

POUFFE:

With 10.00mm (UK 000) hook and B, make 5ch, join with a ss into first ch to form a ring.

1st round: 3ch (counts as first tr), 11tr into ring, join with a ss into 3rd of 3ch. 12tr.

2nd round: 3ch, miss st at base of ch, 2tr into each tr to end, 1tr into st at base of 3ch and changing to C, join with a ss into 3rd of 3ch. 24tr.

3rd round: With C, 3ch, miss st at base of ch, 2tr into next tr, (1tr into foll tr, 2tr into next tr) 11 times, changing to D, join with a ss into 3rd of 3ch. 36tr.

4th round: With D, 3ch, miss st at base of ch, 1tr into foll tr, 2tr into next tr, (1tr into each of foll 2tr, 2tr into next tr) 11 times, changing to A, join with a ss into 3rd of 3ch. 48tr.

5th round: With A, 3ch, miss st at base of ch, 1tr into each of foll 2tr, 2tr into next tr, (1tr into each of foll 3tr, 2tr into next tr) 11 times, changing to E, join with a ss into 3rd of 3ch. 60tr.

6th round: With E, 3ch, miss st at base of ch, 1tr into each of foll 3tr, 2tr into next tr, (1tr into each of foll 4tr, 2tr into next tr) 11 times, join with a ss into 3rd of 3ch. 72tr.

7th round: 3ch, miss st at base of ch, 1tr into each of foll 4tr, 2tr into next tr, (1tr into each of foll 5tr, 2tr into next tr) 11 times, changing to F, join with a ss into 3rd of 3ch. 84tr.

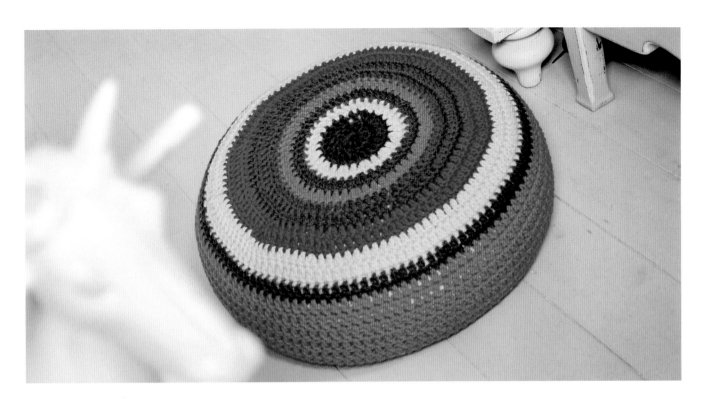

8th round: With F, 3ch, miss st at base of ch, 1tr into each of foll 5tr, 2tr into next tr, (1tr into each of foll 6tr, 2tr into next tr) 11 times, join with a ss into 3rd of 3ch. 96tr.

9th round: 3ch, miss st at base of ch, 1tr into each of foll 6tr, 2tr into next tr, (1tr into each of foll 7tr, 2tr into next tr) 11 times, changing to C, join with a ss into 3rd of 3ch. 108tr.

10th round: With C, 3ch, miss st at base of ch, 1tr into each of foll 7tr, 2tr into next tr, (1tr into each of foll 8tr, 2tr into next tr) 11 times, join with a ss into 3rd of 3ch. 120tr.

11th–21st rounds: Cont in tr without increasing, changing to new colour on last st in old colour. Work 1 round each in C and D, then 9 rounds in A, changing to E on last st of 21st round.

22nd round: With E, 3ch, miss st at base of ch, 1tr into each of next 7tr, tr2tog, (1tr into each of next 8tr, tr2tog) 11 times, join with a ss into 3rd of 3ch. 108tr.

23rd round: 3ch, miss st at base of ch, 1tr into each of next 6tr, tr2tog, (1tr into each of next 7tr, tr2tog) 11 times, changing to F, join with a ss into 3rd of 3ch. 96tr.

24th round: With F, 3ch, miss st at base of ch, 1tr into each of next 5tr, tr2tog, (1tr into each of next 6tr, tr2tog) 11 times, changing to B, join with a ss into 3rd of 3ch. 84tr.

Insert bag of filling.

25th round: With B, 3ch, miss st at base of ch, 1tr into each of next 4tr, tr2tog, (1tr into each of next 5tr, tr2tog) 11 times, join with a ss into 3rd of 3ch. 72tr.

26th round: 3ch, miss st at base of ch, 1tr into each of next 3tr, tr2tog, (1tr into each of next 4tr, tr2tog) 11 times, changing to C, join with a ss into 3rd of 3ch. 60tr.

27th round: With C, 3ch, miss st at base of ch, 1tr into each of next 2tr, tr2tog, (1tr into each of next 3tr, tr2tog) 11 times, join with a ss into 3rd of 3ch. 48tr.

28th round: 3ch, miss st at base of ch, 1tr into next tr, tr2tog, (1tr into each of next 2tr, tr2tog) 11 times, changing to D, join with a ss into 3rd of 3ch. 36tr.

29th round: With D, 3ch, miss st at base of ch, tr2tog, (1tr into next tr, tr2tog) 11 times, changing to F, join with a ss into 3rd of 3ch. 24tr.

30th round: With F, 3ch, miss st at base of ch, 1tr in next tr, (tr2tog) to end, join with a ss into 3rd of 3ch. 12tr.

31st round: As 30th. 6 sts. Fasten off, leaving a 30cm (12in) tail.

Thread yarn tail through a large tapestry needle. Pass needle through back loop only of each st in final round, draw up tightly and fasten off securely.

Patterned socks

Cosy toes are assured with these brightly striped socks.

These pretty socks, worked in a colourful variegated yarn, have a plain foot with a patterned top featuring bullion knots, plus a frilled edging.

GETTING STARTED

⭐⭐⭐ *Making socks requires concentration because of the unusual construction.*

Size:
To fit a woman's foot length 22–26cm (8¾–10¼in) (adjustable)

How much yarn:
1 x 100g (3½oz) ball of King Cole Mirage DK in Marseilles (shade 872)

Hooks:
3.50mm (UK 9) crochet hook
5.00mm (UK 6) crochet hook

Tension:
18 sts and 16 rows measures 10cm (4in) square over main patt on 3.50mm (UK 9) hook
IT IS ESSENTIAL TO WORK TO THE STATED TENSION TO ACHIEVE SUCCESS

What you have to do:
Start at top of leg and work in rounds of bullion stitch pattern, then continue in rounds of main pattern (alternate rounds of half treble and double crochet). Shape heel in double crochet and rows as directed. Pick up stitches for foot from end of heel and continue in rounds, shaping as directed and finally shaping toe. Neaten top of leg with picot border.

The Yarn
King Cole Mirage DK (approx. 312m/340 yards per 100g/3½oz ball) is a practical blend of 50% wool and 50% acrylic. It is machine washable – essential for socks – and there is a large range of variegated shades.

Instructions

Abbreviations:

beg = beginning
BS = bullion st: wind yarn loosely 5 times round hook, insert as directed, yrh and draw a loop through, yrh and draw through all 7 loops
ch = chain(s)
cm = centimetre(s)
cont = continue
dc = double crochet
dc2tog = into each of next 2 sts work: (insert hook into st, yrh and draw through a loop), yrh and draw through all 3 loops on hook
dec = decrease
foll = follow(s)(ing)
htr = half treble
htr2tog = into each of next 2 sts work: (yrh, insert hook into st, yrh and draw through a loop), yrh and draw through all 5 loops on hook
patt = pattern
rem = remaining
rep = repeat
RS = right side
ss = slip stitch
st(s) = stitch(es)
WS = wrong side
yrh = yarn round hook

Note: For second sock to match exactly, wind off yarn as required in order to start at same point in colour sequence.

SOCKS: (make 2)

With 5.00mm (UK 6) hook make 43ch. Change to 3.50mm (UK 9) hook.

Foundation row: 1dc in 3rd ch from hook, 1dc in each ch to end. 42 sts. Join into a ring without twisting, working 1ss in 2nd of 2ch at beg of previous row.

Next round: 1ch (counts as first dc), 1dc in each dc to end, join with a ss in first ch.

Cont in bullion st patt as foll:

1st patt round: 2ch (counts as first htr), miss st at base of ch, *BS in next dc, 1htr in foll dc, rep from * ending BS in last dc, join with a ss in 2nd of 2ch.

2nd patt round: 1ch, miss first BS, *1dc in next htr, 1dc in foll BS, rep from * to end, 1dc under ss at base of first ch, join with a ss in first ch.

(**Note:** Working dc round in this unusual way prevents work from twisting out of true.)

Rep last 2 patt rounds 4 more times, then

work 1st patt round again. 13 rows/rounds in all.

Dec round: 1ch, miss first BS, 1dc in each of next 2 sts, (dc2tog over next 2 sts, 1dc in each of foll 5 sts) 5 times, dc2tog over next 2 sts, 1dc in foll st, 1dc under ss at base of first ch, join with a ss in first ch. 36 sts.

Cont in main patt as foll:

1st round: 2ch, miss st at base of ch, 1htr in each st to end, join with a ss in 2nd of 2ch.

2nd round: 1ch, miss st at base of ch and first htr, 1dc in each htr to end, 1dc under ss at base of first ch, join with a ss in first ch.

Rep these 2 rounds once more, then work first of them again. Fasten off.

Shape heel:

With RS of work facing, rejoin yarn to 9th htr before end of previous round.

1st heel row: 1ch, dc2tog over next 2 sts, 1dc in each of foll 12 sts, dc2tog over next 2 sts, 1dc in next st, turn. 16 sts.

2nd heel row: 1ch, miss st at base of ch, 1dc in each st to end, working last dc in 1ch, turn.

3rd heel row: 1ch, miss st at base of ch, dc2tog over next 2 sts, 1dc in each dc to last 3 sts, dc2tog over next 2 sts, 1dc in 1ch, turn. 14 sts.

Rep 2nd and 3rd heel rows 3 more times, then work 2nd heel row again, ending with a WS row. 8 sts; 10 heel rows.

11th heel row: 1ch, miss st at base of ch, 2dc in next dc, 1dc in each dc to last 2 sts, 2dc in next dc, 1dc in 1ch, turn. 10 sts.

12th heel row: As 2nd heel row.

Rep last 2 heel rows 4 more times, ending with a WS row. 18 sts; 20 heel rows.

Fasten off.

Foot:

With RS of work facing, rejoin yarn to 10th st of last heel row.

Next round: 1ch, 1dc in each of rem 8 sts of last heel row, miss side edge of heel shaping, 1dc in same place as last st of 1st heel row, 1dc in each of 18 sts, 1dc in same place as first st of 1st heel row, miss side edge of heel shaping, 1dc in each of rem 9dc of last heel row, join with a ss in first ch. 38 sts. Work 2 rounds in main patt.

1st foot dec round: 2ch, miss st at base of ch, 1htr in each of next 7dc, htr2tog over next 2dc, 1htr in each of next 18dc, htr2tog over next 2dc, 1htr in each of next 8dc, join with a ss in 2nd of 2ch. 36 sts.

2nd foot dec round: As 2nd patt round.

3rd foot dec round: 2ch, miss st at base of ch, 1htr in each of next 6dc, htr2tog over next 2dc, 1htr in each of next 18dc, htr2tog over next 2dc, 1htr in each of next 7dc, join with a ss in 2nd of 2ch. 34 sts.

4th foot dec round: As 2nd patt round.

5th foot dec round: 2ch, miss st at base of ch, 1htr in each of next 5dc, htr2tog over next 2dc, 1htr in each of next 18dc, htr2tog over next 2dc, 1htr in each of next

6dc, join with a ss in 2nd of 2ch. 32 sts. Cont in main patt, beg with 2nd round, until foot measures 1.5cm (⅝in) less than foot length required, ending with a 1st round.

Shape toe:

1st toe round: 1ch, 1dc in each of next 5htr, (dc2tog over next 2htr) twice, 1dc in each of next 12htr, (dc2tog over next 2htr) twice, 1dc in each of next 6htr, join with a ss in first ch. 28 sts.

2nd toe round: 1ch, 1dc in each of next 4dc, (dc2tog over next 2dc) twice, 1dc in each of next 10dc, (dc2tog over next 2dc) twice, 1dc in each of next 5dc, join with a ss in first ch. 24 sts.

3rd toe round: 1ch, 1dc in each of next 3dc, (dc2tog over next 2dc) twice, 1dc in each of next 8dc, (dc2tog over next 2dc) twice, 1dc in each of next 4dc, join with a ss in first ch. 20 sts.

4th toe round: 1ch, 1dc in each of next 2dc, (dc2tog over next 2dc) twice, 1dc in each of next 6dc, (dc2tog over next 2dc) twice, 1dc in each of next 3dc, join with a ss in first ch. 16 sts. Fasten off.

Top border:

With RS of work facing, rejoin yarn at centre back to base of first st in foundation round.

1st round: 1ch, miss st at base of ch, 1dc in base of each st all around, join with a ss in first ch. 42 sts.

2nd round: 5ch, ss in 3rd ch from hook, (BS, 3ch, ss in 3rd ch from hook) in each dc all around, join with a ss in 2nd of 5ch. Fasten off.

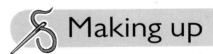

Making up

Join heel seams, then join toe seam.

Rainbow-edged throw

Traditional white lacy squares are edged with bright colours to give a throw with a difference.

Worked in a soft and cosy cotton yarn, this stunning throw has a traditional centre panel with large white lacy squares but it has been given a contemporary twist with brightly coloured edgings in a simple trebles format.

The Yarn

Rico Creative Cotton Aran (approx. 85m/93 yards per 50g/1¾oz ball) is 100% cotton. It is a softly spun yarn that gives good stitch definition and there is a good colour range.

GETTING STARTED

★★★ *Making this throw involves a lot of work but it is well worth the effort.*

Size:
137 x 110cm (54 x 43½in)

How much yarn:
9 x 50g (1¾oz) balls of Rico Creative Cotton Aran in colour A – White (shade 80)
4 balls in colour B – Nougat (shade 56)
2 balls in each of six other colours:
C – Yellow (shade 63); D – Tangerine (shade 76);
E – Fuchsia (shade 13); F – Pistachio (shade 41);
G – Cardinal (shade 11); H – Jeans-light
(shade 27)

Hook:
5.00mm (UK 6) crochet hook

Tension:
One motif (9 rounds) measures 23cm (9in) square on 5.00mm (UK 6) hook
IT IS ESSENTIAL TO WORK TO THE STATED TENSION TO ACHIEVE SUCCESS

What you have to do:
Work 12 lacy square motifs for centre panel, each with a different coloured edging. Crochet square motifs together to form centre panel. Work multicoloured border with groups of three trebles around centre panel. Work scalloped edging around entire throw.

Instructions

Abbreviations:

ch = chain(s)
cl(s) = cluster(s)
cm = centimetre(s)
cont = continue
dc = double crochet
dtr = double treble
foll = follow(s)(ing)
gr(s) = group(s)
patt = pattern
rep = repeat
RS = right side
sp(s) = spaces(s)
ss = slip stitch
st(s) = stitch(es)
tr = treble
WS = wrong side
yrh = yarn round hook

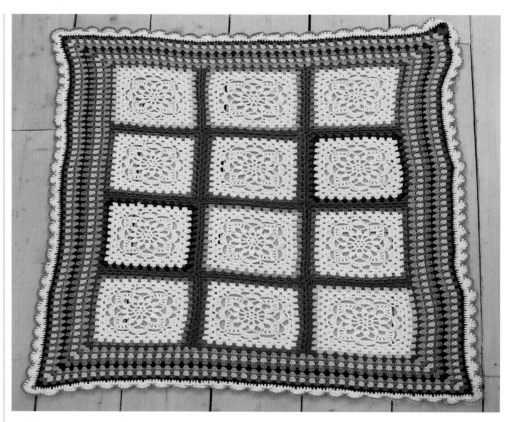

THROW:

Lacy motif: (make 12)
With 5.00mm (UK 6) hook and A, make 6ch.

1st round: In 6th ch from hook, work 1tr, (2ch, 1tr in same ch) 4 times, 2ch, join with a ss in 3rd of first 5ch. 6tr and 6 ch sps.

2nd round: Ss in next ch sp, 6ch (counts as 1dtr and 2ch), 1dtr in same ch sp, *2ch, (1dtr, 2ch, 1dtr) in next ch sp, rep from * 4 times more, 2ch, join with a ss in 4th of 6ch. 12dtr and 12 ch sps.

3rd round: Ss in next ch sp, 3ch (counts as first tr), leaving last loop of each on hook work 3tr in same ch sp, yrh and draw through all 4 loops on hook – counts as first tr cl, *6ch, leaving last loop of each on hook work 4tr in next ch sp, yrh and draw through all 5 loops on hook – called 1 cl, rep from * 10 times more, 3ch, join with a tr in top of first cl, 1ch, 1dc in top of last tr.

4th round: *In next ch sp work (1dtr, 1ch) 6 times, 1dtr – for first corner; 1dc in next ch sp, 6ch, 1dc in next ch sp, rep from * 3 times more, omitting dc at end of last rep and joining with a ss in dc at end of 3rd round.

5th round: *6ch, 1dc in 4th of 7dtr, 4ch, ss in same dtr; 6ch, 1dc in next dc, 5tr in next ch sp, 1dc in next dc, rep from * 3 times more, working last dc in ss at end of 4th round.

6th round: Ss in first 6ch sp, 3ch (counts as first tr), 5tr in same sp, 5tr in 4ch loop, 6tr in next 6ch sp, *3ch, 1dc in 3rd of next 5tr, 3ch, 6tr in next 6ch sp, 5tr in 4ch loop, 6tr in next 6ch sp, rep from * twice more, 3ch, 1dc in 3rd of next 5tr, 3ch, join

with a ss in 3rd of 3ch.

7th round: Turn work so that WS is facing, ss in first 3ch sp, 3ch (counts as first tr), 2tr in same sp, 3tr in next 3ch sp, *3tr in sp between 3rd and 4th tr of next 6tr gr, 3tr in sp between 6tr gr and 5tr gr at corner, (3tr, 2ch, 3tr) in 3rd of 5tr, 3tr in sp between 5tr gr and next 6tr gr, 3tr in sp between 3rd and 4th tr of next 6tr gr, (3tr in next 3ch sp) twice, rep from * twice more, 3tr in sp between 3rd and 4th tr of next 6tr gr, 3tr in sp between 6tr gr and 5tr gr at corner, (3tr, 2ch, 3tr) in 3rd of 5tr, 3tr in sp between 5tr gr and next 6tr gr, 3tr in sp between 3rd and 4th tr of next 6tr gr, join with a ss in 3rd of 3ch.

8th round: Turn work so that RS is facing, ss in sp between first and last 3tr grs, 3ch (counts as first tr), 2tr in same sp, work 3tr in sp between each set of 3tr grs and (3tr, 2ch, 3tr) in each 2ch sp at corners, join with a ss in 3rd of 3ch. Fasten off.

9th round: Join C in any sp between 3tr grs and work as given for 8th round. Fasten off.

Make one more motif using same colour sequence and then 2 motifs each, replacing C in 9th round with D, E, F, G and H (12 motifs in total).

Centre panel:
Arrange lacy motifs in three rows of four motifs with coloured edges in foll sequence (Motif 1 is at top right-hand corner and Motif 12 is at bottom left-hand corner):

1st row: (1) C; (2) H; (3) G; (4) F
2nd row: (5) E; (6) D; (7) E; (8) D
3rd row: (9) F; (10) G; (11) H; (12) C

Joining motifs:
1st row: Motif 1:
10th round: With RS facing and B, work as 9th round.
Motif 2:
10th round: With RS facing, join B to corner 2ch sp,

3ch, 2tr in corner 2ch sp, work as 9th round until 3 sides have been worked, ending 3tr in corner 2ch sp.

With WS facing, work 1dc in corner 2ch sp of Motif 1, 1ch, 3tr in corner 2ch sp of Motif 2, (1dc in sp between 3tr grs on Motif 1, 3tr in sp between 3tr grs on Motif 2) along 4th side, ending 1dc in sp between 3tr grs on Motif 1, 3tr in corner 2ch sp on Motif 2, 1dc in corner 2ch sp on Motif 1, 1ch, ss in 3rd of 3ch on Motif 2. Fasten off.

In same way, join Motif 3 to Motif 2 and Motif 4 to Motif 3.

2nd row: Motif 5:
10th round: Work as given for Motif 2 joining 4th side to Motif 1 of 1st row.

Motif 6:
10th round: Work as given for Motif 2 but work along 2 sides only, ending 3tr in corner 2ch sp. Join 3rd side to Motif 5 as before.

At corner work 1dc in 2ch sp at corner of Motif 5, then 1dc in 2ch sp at corner of Motif 2 of 1st row, 3tr in corner 2ch sp of Motif 6, join 4th side to Motif 2 of 1st row as before. Fasten off.

Multicoloured border:
With 5.00mm (UK 6) hook and RS of work facing, join D to any corner sp, 3ch, 2tr in same sp, cont around sides of centre panel working 3tr in each sp and (3tr, 2ch, 3tr) in each corner sp, ending 3tr in corner sp, 2ch, join with a ss in 3rd of 3ch. Fasten off.

Work 10 more rounds in same way in stripe sequence as foll: 1 round each H, C, E, F, G, D, H, C, E and G.

Edging:
Next round: Join A to same place as ss at end of last round, 3ch (counts as first tr), miss st at base of ch, 1tr in each tr around all sides, working 4ch at each corner, join with a ss in 3rd of 3ch.

Next round: Ss in each of next 2tr, 1dc in sp before next tr, *(miss 3tr, (1dtr, 1ch) 5 times in sp between tr, miss 3tr, 1dc in sp between tr) to last 3tr, (1dtr, 1ch) 9 times in 4ch sp at corner, miss 3tr, 1dc in sp between tr, rep from * 3 times more omitting last dc, join with a ss in first dc. Fasten off.

Next round: Join F to sp after any 5dtr fan, 1ch (counts as first dc), *ss in next dc, 1dc in sp before next 5dtr fan, (1ch, 1dc in sp between next 2 sts) 5 times, rep from * all round, working instructions in brackets 9 times at each corner, join with a ss in 1ch. Fasten off.

Openwork hat

This 1920s-style hat could be adapted for evening wear if you used a glittery yarn.

This close-fitting cloche-style hat is made in a soft yarn using a pretty openwork pattern with scallops around the face. It also features a plain band trimmed with a decorative button.

GETTING STARTED

 Experience of working in rounds would be an advantage.

Size:

To fit an average-sized woman's head

How much yarn:

2 x 50g (1¾oz) balls of Artesano Inca Mist DK in Cinnamon (shade 0180)

Hook:

4.00mm (UK 8) crochet hook

Additional item:

Large decorative button, needle and matching thread

Tension:

2 reps of patt measure 7.5cm (3in) and 10 rows measure 10cm (4in) over patt on 4.00mm (UK 8) hook

IT IS ESSENTIAL TO WORK TO THE STATED TENSION TO ACHIEVE SUCCESS

What you have to do:

Work hat entirely in rounds, shaping as directed. Work crown section in trebles and remainder in openwork pattern with lacy shells to give a scalloped edge to hat. Make a strip in rows of double crochet and join to form a band. Sew on button to cover join of band.

The Yarn

Artesano Inca Mist DK (approx. 120m/132 yards per 50g/1¾oz ball) contains 100% baby alpaca. It is soft and luxurious with a slight twist, and is hand washable. There is a small but lovely range of colours.

Instructions

Abbreviations:

ch = chain(s)

cm = centimetre(s)

cont = continue

dc = double crochet

foll = follows

patt = pattern

rep = repeat

sp = space

ss = slip stitch

st(s) = stitch(es)

tr = treble

WS = wrong side

Note: To make a Magic Circle, wrap yarn clockwise around forefinger twice to form a ring. Holding end of yarn between thumb and middle finger, insert hook into ring and draw yarn from ball through.

HAT:

With 4.00mm (UK 8) hook make a magic circle (see Note left) and work as foll:

1st round: 3ch (counts as first tr), work 11 tr into ring, join with a ss into 3rd of 3ch. 12 sts.

2nd round: 3ch, 1tr into st at base of ch, 2tr into each st all round, join with a ss into 3rd of 3ch. 24 sts.

3rd round: 3ch, 1tr into st at base of ch, 1tr into next st, *2tr into next st, 1tr into next st, rep from * to end, join with a ss into 3rd of 3ch. 36 sts.

4th round: 3ch, 1tr into st at base of ch, 1tr into each of next 2 sts, *2tr into next st, 1tr into each of next 2 sts, rep from * to end, join with a ss into 3rd of 3ch. 48 sts.

5th round: 3ch, 1tr into st at base of ch, 1tr into each of next 3 sts, *2tr into next st, 1tr into each of next 3 sts, rep from * to end, join with a ss into 3rd of 3ch. 60 sts.

Cont in patt as foll:

Next round: 3ch, miss st at base of ch, 1tr into next st, miss next st, (3tr, 1ch, 3tr) into

next st, miss next st, *1tr into each of next 2 sts, miss next st, (3tr, 1ch, 3tr) into next st, miss next st, rep from * to end, join with a ss into 3rd of 3ch.

Patt round: 3ch, miss st at base of ch, 1tr into next st, (3tr, 1ch, 3tr) into next 1ch sp, *miss next 3 sts, 1tr into each of next 2 sts, (3tr, 1ch, 3tr) into next 1ch sp, rep from * to end, join with a ss into 3rd of 3ch.

Rep last round 12 times more. Fasten off.

BAND:

With 4.00mm (UK 8) hook make 101ch.

Foundation row: (WS) 1dc into 2nd ch from hook, 1dc into each ch to end, turn. 100 sts.

Patt row: 1ch (does not count as a st), working into back loop only, 1dc into each st to end, turn.

Rep last row 10 times more. Fasten off.

 # Making up

Join short ends of band, then sew on button to cover seam. Fit band over hat as shown and either leave loose or secure to hat with a few stitches.

Lacy bed cushion

Old-fashioned charm plus a crisp, linear stitch pattern makes an elegant pillow.

Complement a feminine bedroom with this decorative cushion cover worked in a fine cotton yarn, pretty openwork pattern and lined in a matching cotton fabric.

GETTING STARTED

 Pattern should be easy to keep correct once established but patience is needed as yarn is quite fine.

Size:
Approximately 45 x 45cm (18 x 18in)

How much yarn:
2 x 100g (3½oz) balls of DMC Petra No. 3 in Ecru

Hook:
2.50mm (UK 12) crochet hook

Additional items:
47 x 92cm (18½ x 36in) rectangle of cream cotton fabric for lining
Matching 40cm (16in) zip fastener
Matching sewing thread
45cm square cushion pad

Tension:
Five 5ch sps and 10 rounds measure 10cm (4in) square over grid patt on Back on 2.50mm (UK 12) hook
IT IS ESSENTIAL TO WORK TO THE STATED TENSION TO ACHIEVE SUCCESS

What you have to do:
Work front in rounds of lacy filet pattern to produce a large openwork square. Work decorative picot edging around outer edge of front. Work back in openwork grid pattern. Sew cotton fabric lining with zippered opening. Slip stitch crochet front and back in place on cotton lining.

 Instructions

FRONT:
With 2.50mm (UK 12) hook make 8ch, join with ss in first ch to form a ring.

1st round: 3ch (counts as first tr), 6tr in ring, (2ch, 7tr in ring) 3 times, 2ch, join with a ss in 3rd of 3ch.

2nd round: 8ch (counts as 1tr, 5ch), *(3tr, 3ch, 3tr) in next 2ch sp, 5ch, rep from * twice more, (3tr, 3ch, 2tr) in last 2ch sp, join with a ss in 3rd of 8ch.***

3rd round: 6ch (counts as 1tr, 3ch), 1dc in 5ch sp, *3ch, 1tr in each of next 3tr, (3tr, 3ch, 3tr) in corner 3ch sp, 1tr in each of next 3tr, 3ch, 1dc in next 5ch sp, rep from * twice more, 3ch, 1tr in each of next 3tr, (3tr, 3ch, 3tr) in corner 3ch sp, 1tr in each of next 2tr, join with a ss in 3rd of 6ch.

The Yarn
DMC Petra No. 3 is a mercerized thread in 100% cotton. It produces a soft and supple fabric that is ideal for decorative projects and as well as neutrals there is a wide range of other fabulous colours to choose from.

Abbreviations:
ch = chain(s)
cm = centimetre(s)
cont = continue
dc = double crochet
patt = pattern
rep(s) = repeat(s)
RS = right side
sp(s) = space(s)
ss = slip stitch
st(s) = stitch(es)
tr = treble

4th round: 8ch, *1tr in each of next 6tr, (3tr, 3ch, 3tr) in corner 3ch sp, 1tr in each of next 6tr, 5ch, rep from * twice more, 1tr in each of next 6tr, (3tr, 3ch, 3tr) in corner 3ch sp, 1tr in each of next 5tr, join with a ss in 3rd of 8ch.

5th round: 6ch, 1dc in 5ch sp, *3ch, 1tr in each of next 9tr, (3tr, 3ch, 3tr) in corner 3ch sp, 1tr in each of next 9tr, 3ch, 1dc in next 5ch sp, rep from * twice more, 3ch, 1tr in each of next 9tr, (3tr, 3ch, 3tr) in corner 3ch sp, 1tr in each of next 8tr, join with a ss in 3rd of 6ch.

6th round: 8ch, *1tr in each of next 12tr, (3tr, 3ch, 3tr) in corner 3ch sp, 1tr in each of next 12tr, 5ch, rep from * twice more, 1tr in each of next 12tr, (3tr, 3ch, 3tr) in corner 3ch sp, 1tr in each of next 11tr, join with a ss in 3rd of 8ch.

7th round: 6ch, 1dc in 5ch sp, *3ch, 1tr in each of next 15tr, (3tr, 3ch, 3tr) in corner 3ch sp, 1tr in each of next 15tr, 3ch, 1dc in next 5ch sp, rep from * twice more, 3ch, 1tr in each of next 15tr, (3tr, 3ch, 3tr) in corner 3ch sp, 1tr in each of next 14tr, join with a ss in 3rd of 6ch.

8th round: 8ch, *1tr in next tr, 5ch, miss 5tr, 1tr in next tr, 1tr in each of next 11tr, (3tr, 3ch, 3tr) in corner 3ch sp, 1tr in each of next 12tr, 5ch, miss 5tr **, 1tr in next tr, 5ch, rep from * 3 times more ending last rep at **, join with a ss in 3rd of 8ch.

9th round: 6ch, 1dc in 5ch sp, 3ch, 1tr in next tr, 3ch, 1dc in 5ch sp, 3ch, 1tr in next tr, *3ch, miss 2tr, 1dc in next tr, 3ch, miss 2tr, 1tr in next tr, 1tr in each of next 8tr, (3tr, 3ch, 3tr) in corner 3ch sp, 1tr in each of next 9tr, 3ch, miss 2tr, 1dc in next tr, 3ch, miss 2tr, 1tr in next tr**, (3ch, 1dc in 5ch sp, 3ch, 1tr in next tr) 3 times, rep from * 3 times more ending last rep at **, 3ch, 1dc in 5ch sp, 3ch, join with a ss in 3rd of 6ch.

10th round: 8ch, 1tr in next tr, (5ch, 1tr in next tr) twice, *5ch, miss 5tr, 1tr in next tr, 1tr in each of next 5tr, (3tr, 3ch, 3tr) in corner 3ch sp, 1tr in each of next 6tr, 5ch, miss 5tr, 1tr in next tr**, (5ch, 1tr in next tr) 5 times, rep from * 3 times more ending last rep at **, 5ch, 1tr in next tr, 5ch, join with a ss in 3rd of 8ch.

11th round: 6ch, 1dc in 5ch sp, 3ch, 1tr in next tr, (3ch, 1dc in 5ch sp, 3ch, 1tr in next tr) 3 times, *3ch, miss 2tr, 1dc in next tr, 3ch, miss 2tr, 1tr in next tr, 1tr in each of next 2tr, (3tr, 3ch, 3tr) in corner 3ch sp, 1tr in each of next 3tr, 3ch, miss 2tr, 1dc in next tr, 3ch, miss 2tr, 1tr in next tr**, (3ch, 1dc in 5ch sp, 3ch, 1tr in next tr) 7 times, rep from * 3 times more ending last rep at **, (3ch, 1dc in 5ch sp, 3ch, 1tr in next tr) twice, 3ch, 1dc in 5ch sp, 3ch, join with a ss in 3rd of 6ch.

12th round: 8ch, 1tr in next tr, *(5ch, 1tr

in next tr) 4 times, 5ch, miss 5 sts, (3tr, 3ch, 3tr) in corner 3ch sp, 5ch, miss 5 sts, 1tr in next tr **, (5ch, 1tr in next tr) 5 times, rep from * 3 times more, ending last rep at **, (5ch, 1tr in next tr) 4 times omitting 1tr at end of last rep, join with a ss in 3rd of 8ch.

13th round: 6ch, 1dc in 5ch sp, 3ch, 1tr in next tr, *(3ch, 1dc in 5ch sp, 3ch, 1tr in next tr) 5 times, 2ch, miss 2tr, (3tr, 3ch, 3tr) in corner 3ch sp, 2ch, miss 2tr, 1tr in next tr **, (3ch, 1dc in 5ch sp, 3ch, 1tr in next tr) 6 times, rep from * 3 times more, ending last rep at **, (3ch, 1dc in 5ch sp, 3ch, 1tr in next tr) 5 times omitting 1tr at end of last rep, join with a ss in 3rd of 6ch.

14th–20th rounds: Rep 12th and 13th rounds 3 times, then work 12th round again, noting that each rep of the 2 rows results in an extra 2 patt reps on each side of square.

21st round: 3ch (counts as first tr), (5tr in next 5ch sp, 1tr in next tr) 10 times, *1tr in each of next 2tr, (3tr, 3ch, 3tr) in corner 3ch sp, 1tr in each of next 3tr, (5tr in next 5ch sp, 1tr in next tr) 19 times, rep from * twice more, 1tr in each of next 2tr, (3tr, 3ch, 3tr) in corner 3ch sp, 1tr in each of next 3tr, (5tr in next 5ch sp, 1tr in next tr) 8 times, 5tr in last 5ch sp, join with a ss in 3rd of 3ch.

22nd round: (**Note** – each dc or (2tr, 3ch, 2tr) group is worked in centre tr of 5tr group of last round.) Ss in each of first 3 sts, 1ch, 1dc in same place as last ss, (3ch, miss 5tr, (2tr, 3ch, 2tr) in next tr, 3ch, miss 5tr, 1dc in next tr) 5 times, *3ch, (3tr, 3ch, 3tr) in corner 3ch sp, 3ch, miss 2tr, 1dc in next tr, (3ch, miss 5tr, (2tr, 3ch, 2tr) in next tr, 3ch, miss 5tr, 1dc in next tr) 10 times, rep from * twice more, 3ch, (3tr, 3ch, 3tr) in corner 3ch sp, 3ch, miss 2tr, 1dc in next tr, (3ch, miss 5tr, (2tr, 3ch, 2tr) in next tr, 3ch, miss 5tr, 1dc in next tr) 5 times omitting 1dc at end of last rep, join with a ss in first dc.

23rd round: *3ch, miss 3ch sp, in next 3ch sp work 1tr, (3ch, ss in first of 3ch, 1tr) 4 times, 3ch, 1dc in next dc, rep from * to end, join with a ss in base of 3ch. Fasten off.

BACK:
Work as for given for Front to ***.

3rd round: 6ch (counts as 1tr, 3ch), *1dc in next 5ch sp, 3ch, 1tr in next tr, 3ch, miss 2tr, (3tr, 3ch, 3tr) in corner 3ch sp, 3ch, miss 2tr**, 1tr in next tr, 3ch, rep from * 3 times more ending last rep at **, join with a ss in 3rd of 6ch.

4th round: 8ch (counts as 1tr, 5ch), *1tr in next tr, 5ch, miss next 3ch sp and 3tr, (3tr, 3ch, 3tr) in corner 3ch sp, 5ch, miss 3tr and 3ch sp**, 1tr in next tr, 5ch, rep from * 3 times more ending last rep at **, join with a ss in 3rd

of 8ch. The last 2 rounds set patt as given for 12th–20th rounds of Front. Cont in patt as now set until 20 rounds have been worked.

21st round: As 21st round of Front. Fasten off.

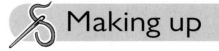

Making up

Fold piece of lining fabric in half widthways with RS facing. Taking a 1cm (⅜in) seam, stitch lower edge for 2cm (¾in) at each side. Press seam open. Sew zip fastener into opening. With RS facing and zip open, sew adjacent side seams. Turn lining RS out. Place cushion front on top of lining and pin in place all round. Using matching sewing thread, slip stitch cushion front to one side of lining, taking care to sew to one side of zip opening only. Place face down and lay cushion back in position on the other side of the lining. Slip stitch in place all round, taking care to sew to opposite side of zip opening. Insert cushion pad.

Fisherman's tea cosy

A strong cuppa is what's required after taking the sea air – this helps to make sure it is nice and hot!

This fabulous quirky cosy is constructed from a textured relief pattern featuring fish motifs, bubbles and waves, while a boat sits atop and nets form the edging around the bottom.

GETTING STARTED

 *The relief pattern takes some crochet skill, as does making the neat decorative elements.*

Size:
When flat, 28cm (11in) wide x 30cm (12in) tall

How much yarn:
3 x 50g (1¾oz) balls of Sirdar Click Chunky in colour A – Marine Blue (shade 165)
1 ball in each of four other colours: B – Canvas (shade 170); C – Cobble (shade 129); D – Wild (shade 112) and E – Really Red (shade 163)

Hook:
6.00mm (UK 4) crochet hook

Additional items:
Polyester toy filling, safety-pins

Tension:
11 sts and 7 rows measure 10cm (4in) square over patt on 6.00mm (UK 4) hook
IT IS ESSENTIAL TO WORK TO THE STATED TENSION TO ACHIEVE SUCCESS

What you have to do:
Work main part of cosy in trebles with relief pattern and bobbles in a contrast colour. Make boat and lifebelt decorations for top of cosy in rounds. Decorate lower edge of cosy with a loop edging.

The Yarn
Sirdar Click Chunky (approx. 75m/82 yards per 50g/1¾oz ball) contains 70% acrylic and 30% wool. It makes it a practical fabric that can be machine washed. It is a good-looking yarn with an interesting colour range including variegated shades.

 ## Instructions

COSY: (make 2)
With 6.00mm (UK 4) hook and A, make 32ch.
Foundation row: (RS) 1dc in 2nd ch from hook, 1dc in each ch to end, turn. 31 sts.
1st row: 2xch (count as first tr), miss st at base of ch, 1tr in each st to end, turn.
2nd row: 2xch, miss st at base of ch, 1tr in each of next 2 sts, *1rdtrf around stem of 2nd st back, miss next st, 1tr in each of next 3 sts, 1rdtrb around stem of 3rd st forward, miss next st**, 1tr in each of next 5 sts*, rep from * to * once more, then work from * to ** again, 1tr in each of next 2 sts, 1tr in top of turning ch, turn.
3rd row: 2xch, miss st at base of ch, 1tr in each of next 4 sts, *leaving last loop of each st on hook work 1rdtrb around each of next 2rdtrf, yrh and draw through all 3 loops, miss next st**, 1tr in each of next 9 sts*, rep from * to * once more, then work from * to ** again, 1tr in each of next 4 sts, 1tr in top of turning ch, turn.
4th row: 2xch, miss st at base of ch, 1tr in each of next 2 sts, *1rdtrf around left stem of joined rdtrb, miss next st, 1tr in each of next 3 sts, 1rdtrf around right stem of joined rdtrb, miss next st**, 1tr in each of next 5 sts*, rep from * to * once more, then work from * to ** again, 1tr in each of next 2 sts, 1tr in top of turning ch, turn.
5th row: 2xch, miss st at base of ch, 1tr in each of next 2 sts, *1rdtrb around stem of rdtrf, 1tr in each of next 3 sts, 1rdtrb around stem of rdtrf**, 1tr in each of next 5tr*, rep from * to * once more, then work from * to ** again, 1tr in each of last 2tr, 1tr in top of turning ch, turn.

Abbreviations:

ch = chain(s)

cm = centimetre(s)

cont = continue

dc = double crochet

foll = follow(s)(ing)

htr = half treble

patt = pattern

Pc = popcorn: 5tr in same st, slip loop off hook, insert hook in top of first tr, replace loop on hook and draw loop through

rdtrb(f) = relief double treble back (front): work 1dtr from right to left and back to front (front to back) around stem of st indicated

rep = repeat

RS = right side

ss = slip stitch

st(s) = stitch(es)

tr = treble

WS = wrong side

xch = extended ch: work slightly longer than a standard ch

yrh = yarn round hook

6th row: 2xch, miss st at base of ch, 1tr in each of next 2tr, *1rdtrf around stem of rdtrb, 1tr in next tr, 1Pc in next tr, 1tr in next tr, 1rdtrf around stem of rdtrb**, 1tr in each of next 5tr*, rep from * to * once more, then work from * to ** again, 1tr in each of next 2tr, 1tr in top of turning ch, turn.

7th row: As 5th row.

8th row: 2xch, miss st at base of ch, 1tr in each of next 4 sts, *leaving last loop of each st on hook work 1rdtrf around stem of each of next 2rdtrb, yrh and draw through all 3 loops, miss next st**, 1tr in each of next 9 sts*, rep from * to * once more, then work from * to ** again, 1tr in each of next 4 sts, 1tr in top of turning ch, turn.

9th row: 2xch, miss st at base of ch, 1tr in each st to end, 1tr in top of turning ch, turn.

Cont in popcorn patt introducing new colour on last pull through of last st in previous colour:

10th row: With A, 2xch, miss st at base of ch, 1tr in each of next 2tr, *1Pc in B, 3tr in A, rep from * 6 times more working final tr in top of turning ch, turn. Fasten off B.

11th row: With A, 2xch, miss st at base of ch, 1tr in each st to end, 1tr in top of turning ch, turn.

12th row: With A, 2xch, miss st at base of ch, 1tr in each of next 4tr, *1Pc in B, 3tr in A, rep from * 5 times more, 1tr in last tr, 1tr in top of turning ch, turn. Fasten off B and cont in A.

13th and 14th rows: As 11th row.

15th row: *4ch, miss 1ch, ss in next ch, 3ch, miss 3 sts, ss in next st*, rep from * to * 6 times, 4ch, miss 1ch, ss in next ch, 3ch, ss in top of turning ch, turn.

Fold last row down onto RS of work and work next row behind these sts.

16th row: 4ch, miss 1ch, ss in next ch, 3ch, miss turning ch of 14th row, ss in next tr, work from * to * of 15th row 7 times, 4ch, miss 1ch, ss in next ch, 3ch, ss in last tr of 14th row.

Fasten off leaving a long tail, thread end into tapestry needle and weave it through top of 14th row to opposite edge so that top can be gathered when making up.

BOAT:

With 6.00mm (UK 4) hook and D, make 9ch.
Worked with WS facing.

1st round: 1dc in 2nd ch from hook, 1dc in each ch to end, 2dc in side of last dc, then work 1dc in each loop along other side of foundation ch, join with a ss in first dc. 18 sts.

2nd round: 2ch (counts as first htr), working in front loop only of each st, *2htr in next st, 1htr in foll st, rep from * to last st, 2htr in last st, join with a ss in 2nd of 2ch. 27 sts.

3rd round: 2ch, 1htr in each st to end, join with a ss in 2nd of 2ch.

4th round: 1ch (counts as first dc), (dc2tog) to end, join with a ss in first ch. Fasten off leaving a long end.

Turn to RS. Stuff boat with toy filling, then slip stitch two long top edges closed, taking yarn end through to lower edge for use in attaching boat to cosy.

With 6.00mm (UK 4) hook and E, make a magic circle (see Note on page 94).
Work with WS facing.

Cabin:

1st round: 3ch (counts as first tr), work 9tr in loop, join with a ss in 3rd of 3ch and tighten loop to close. 10 sts.

2nd round: 1ch (counts as first dc), working in front loop only, 1dc in st at base of ch, 1dc in each st to end,

join with a ss in first ch. 11 sts.

3rd round: Work 1 more round in dc, working in both loops of each st. Fasten off leaving a long end. Turn to RS. Stuff with toy filling and sew this section to centre top of boat. Join C to st at centre of one end of boat, (take yarn tightly along first side and through one st at centre of other end, take yarn tightly along second side and through st at joining point) twice. Fasten off.

Lifebelt:

With 6.00mm (UK 4) hook and E, make 5ch, join with a ss in first ch to form a ring.

1st round: 1ch, work 10dc in ring, join with a ss in first dc. Fasten off leaving a long end.

Wrap two lengths of B several times around ring as shown in picture, securing neatly on WS. Sew top of lifebelt to outer edge of boat.

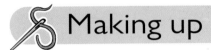 ## Making up

Place two cosy sections with WS facing. Slip stitch side edges together for 7cm (2¾in) up from lower edge at each side. Also slip stitch down for 7cm (2¾in) from base of waves.

Using long ends woven through base of waves, pull up and gather top edge of cosy and fasten off securely. (There will be a small gap at top of cosy where the boat will sit.) Position boat as required (using safety pins if preferred), ensuring all waves are fanned out away from boat. Secure one corner of boat to edge of cosy, then carefully turn inside out with base of boat facing. Sew around edge of boat, catching to base of waves as you go. Turn cosy RS out.

Net edging:

With 6.00mm (UK 4) hook and RS facing, join C to lower edge at one side seam.

1st round: *5ch, miss next st, ss in base of next st, rep from * to last st, 2ch, 1tr in first ch of round.

2nd round: *5ch, ss in next loop, rep from * ending 5ch, ss in loop formed by 2ch and 1tr. Fasten off.

Scalloped lace collar

Pretty collars such as this are always on trend; add one to a plain jumper or dress.

Based on a traditional design, this detachable collar fastens with a button and features pretty lace motifs with a scalloped edging.

GETTING STARTED

★★ *Crocheted in small easy motifs joined as you work.*

Size:
To fit an adult; depth at centre back 6cm (2⅜ in) (including neckband)

How much yarn:
1 x 50g (1¾oz) ball of Anchor Style Creativa Fino in White (shade 1331)

Hook:
2.50mm (UK 12) crochet hook

Additional item:
Small round button

Tension:
First motif measures 10.5cm (4⅛ in) across straight edge x 5cm (2in) deep on 2.50mm (UK 12) hook
IT IS ESSENTIAL TO WORK TO THE STATED TENSION TO ACHIEVE SUCCESS

What you have to do:
Begin with semi-circular motif for centre back, then crochet three smaller motifs at each side, joining as you work. Motifs have five rows, beginning with a row of trebles worked into a ring, gradually increasing by working chain spaces between trebles and finishing with a shell edging. Work neckband along straight top edge and fasten with a small button.

The Yarn
Anchor Style Creativa Fino 125m/136 yards per 50g/1¾oz ball) contains 100% mercerized cotton yarn in a 4-ply weight. It produces a smooth fabric with a silky sheen. It is available in a wide range of good colours.

Instructions

Abbreviations:

ch = chain
cm = centimetre(s)
dc = double crochet
dtr = double treble
RS = right side
sp = space
ss = slip stitch
st(s) = stitch(es)
tr = treble
WS = wrong side

COLLAR:
1st motif (centre back):
With 2.50mm (UK 12) hook make 11ch, join with a ss in first ch to form a ring.
1st row: (RS) 3ch (counts as first tr), 11tr in ring, turn. 12 sts.
2nd row: 4ch (counts as 1tr and 1ch), miss tr at base of ch, (1tr in next tr, 1ch) 10 times, 1tr in top of 3ch, turn.
3rd row: 5ch (counts as 1tr and 2ch), miss tr at base of ch, (1tr in next tr, 2ch) 10 times, 1tr in 3rd of 4ch, turn.

4th row: 6ch (counts as 1tr and 3ch), miss tr at base of ch, (1tr in next tr, 3ch) 10 times, 1tr in 3rd of 5ch, turn.
Edging row: (1dc, 3tr, 1dc – 1 shell) in each 3ch sp, turn.
2nd motif:
8ch, join with a ss in centre tr of first shell of edging row on previous motif to form a ring, turn.
1st row: (RS) 3ch (counts as first tr), 8tr in ring, turn. 9 sts.
2nd row: 4ch (counts as 1tr and 1ch), miss tr at base of ch, (1tr in next tr, 1ch) 7 times, 1tr in top of 3ch, join with a ss in centre tr of 2nd shell of edging row on previous motif, turn.
3rd row: 5ch (counts as 1tr and 2ch), miss tr at base of ch, (1tr in next tr, 2ch) 7 times, 1tr in 3rd of 4ch, turn.
4th row: 6ch (counts as 1tr and 3ch), miss tr at base of ch, (1tr in next tr, 3ch) 7 times, 1tr in 3rd of 5ch, join with a ss in centre tr of 3rd shell of edging row on previous motif, turn.
Edging row: 1 shell in each 3ch sp, turn.
3rd and 4th motifs:
Work as given for 2nd motif. Fasten off.
5th motif:
With WS facing, join yarn to centre tr of last shell of edging row on first motif, 4ch,

join with a ss in centre tr of 3rd shell of edging row on first motif, turn.

4th row: 3ch (forms first 3ch sp of row), miss first tr, (1tr in next tr, 3ch) 7 times, 1tr in 3rd of 5ch, turn.

Edging row: 1 shell in each 3ch sp. Fasten off and turn.

6th and 7th motifs: Work as given for 5th motif, joining yarn to previous motif each time and working ss on 1st and 3rd rows in previous motif.

Neckband:

With 2.50mm (UK 12) hook and RS facing, join a short length of yarn to first dc of first shell of edging row on 7th motif, make 4ch. Fasten off.

With RS facing, join yarn to last dc of last shell of edging row on 4th motif, 5ch, 1dc in 2nd ch from hook, 1dc in each of next 3ch, into straight edge of each of first 3 motifs work: (1dc in edging row, 2dc in each of next 4 rows, 3dc in ch ring); across first motif work: (1dc in edging row, 2dc in each of next 4 rows, 3dc in ch ring, 2dc in each of next 4 rows, 1dc in edging row); in each of last 3 motifs work: (3dc in ch ring, 2dc in each of next 4 rows, 1dc in edging row), 1dc in each of 4ch, turn. 101dc.

Next row: 1ch, 1dc in each dc to last 4dc, 3ch, miss 3dc, 1dc in last dc, turn.

Next row: 1ch, 1dc in first dc, 1dc in each of 3ch, 1dc in each dc to end. Fasten off.

 Making up

Darn in ends. Sew on button.

miss next tr, 1dtr in end dc, turn.

1st row: (RS) 3ch, 8tr in 4ch sp, 3ch (forms first tr on next row), join with a ss in centre tr of 2nd shell of edging row on first motif, turn.

2nd row: 1ch (forms first 1ch sp of row), miss first tr, (1tr in next tr, 1ch) 7 times, 1tr in 3rd of 3ch, turn.

3rd row: 5ch, miss tr at base of ch, (1tr in next tr, 2ch) 7 times, 1tr in 3rd of 3ch, 3ch (forms first tr on next row),

Twisted headband

There is a touch of the 1920s about this retro headband with its decorative flower on the side.

Worked in a luxurious Aran yarn and chunky relief stitches, this distinctive headband has a crossover section and is trimmed with loopy flower motifs.

GETTING STARTED

 Working in relief trebles takes practice.

Size:
Headband measures about 50cm (20in) wide x 10cm (4in) deep

How much yarn:
2 x 50g (1¾oz) balls of Debbie Bliss Cashmerino Aran in Plum (shade 17)

Hooks:
5.00mm (UK 6) crochet hook
6.50mm (UK 3) crochet hook

Additional items:
2 small buttons and 2 beads for flower centres

Tension:
17 sts and 10 rows measure 10cm (4in) square over patt on 6.50mm (UK 3) hook
IT IS ESSENTIAL TO WORK TO THE STATED TENSION TO ACHIEVE SUCCESS

What you have to do:
Work throughout in pattern of relief trebles. Work one third of headband, divide and work next third in two separate sections, cross sections over and complete final third as one piece. Make loopy chain-stitch flowers as embellishments and sew onto headband.

The Yarn
Debbie Bliss Cashmerino Aran (approx. 90m/98 yards per 50g/1¾oz ball) contains 55% merino wool, 33% microfibre and 12% cashmere. It produces a soft, luxurious fabric, which can be machine washed but only at a low temperature. There are plenty of great colours to choose from.

Instructions

Abbreviations:

ch = chain
cm = centimetre(s)
cont = continue
dc = double crochet
foll = following
patt = pattern
rep = repeat
RS = right side
rtrb = relief tr back: inserting hook from right to left and from back to front, work 1tr around stem of next st
rtrf = relief tr front: inserting hook from right to left and from front to back, work 1tr around stem of next st
st(s) = stitch(es)
tr = treble
WS = wrong side

HEADBAND:

With 6.50mm (UK 3) hook make 19ch.
Foundation row: (WS) 1tr into 4th ch from hook, 1tr into each ch to end, turn. 17 sts.
1st row: 3ch (counts as first tr), miss st at base of ch, (1rtrf around stem of next st, 1rtrb around stem of foll st) to end, working last rtrb around turning ch, turn.
2nd row: 3ch, miss st at base of ch, (1rtrb around stem of next st, 1rtrf around stem of foll st) to end, working last rtrf around turning ch, turn.
The last 2 rows form patt. Rep them until 15 patt rows in all have completed, ending with a RS row.

First section:

Next row: 3ch, miss st at base of ch, (1rtrb around stem of next st, 1rtrf around stem of foll st) 4 times, turn.

of first section, 3ch, miss st at base of ch, (1rtrb around stem of next st, 1rtrf around stem of foll st) to end, turn. Cont on these 9 sts only for second section, work 20 more rows in patt. Fasten off.

Join sections:
Cross first section over second section and return hook to working loop.

Next row: (RS) 3ch, miss st at base of ch, (1rtrf around stem of next st, 1rtrb around stem of foll st) 3 times, 1rtrf around stem of next st, 1rtrb around stem of last st of first section and around stem of first st of second section together, (1rtrf around stem of next st, 1rtrb around stem of foll st) to end, turn. 17 sts.
Work 15 more rows in patt across joined sts of both sections. Fasten off.

FLOWERS:
Large flower:
With 5.00mm (UK 6) hook make a magic circle (see Note on page 94).
1st round: (20ch, 1dc into ring) 30 times. Fasten off and pull end of yarn to draw ring tight.

Small flower:
With 5.00mm (UK 6) hook make a magic circle.
1st round: (10ch, 1dc into ring) 15 times. Fasten off and pull end of yarn to draw ring tight.

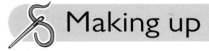 Making up

Join centre back seam. If headband is looser than required, join a row or two at centre at start of opening. Using photograph as a guide, sew on flowers, adding a button with a bead to the centre of each one.

Cont on these 9 sts only for first section, work 20 more rows in patt, ending with a WS row.
Extend loop on hook and remove hook.
Second section:
With WS facing, rejoin yarn to last st worked into at base

Retro bow sweater

Swing into 1950s style with this cute spike-pattern sweater.

Fun and flirty, with its bow-trimmed, off-the-shoulder neckline, this retro-style sweater is worked in a clever yet easy spike-stitch pattern. Contrasting borders give it extra impact.

GETTING STARTED

★★ *Mainly straightforward pattern but concentration is required for working spike-stitch pattern rows.*

Size:
To fit bust: 81[86:91:97]cm (32[34:36:38]in)
Actual size: 85[91:97:103]cm (33½[36:38:40½]in)
Length: 45[45:49:49]cm (17¾[17¾:19¼:19¼]in)
Sleeve seam: 26.5cm (10½in)
Note: Figures in square brackets [ ] refer to larger sizes; where there is only one set of figures, it applies to all sizes

How much yarn:
9[9:10:11] x 50g (1¾oz) balls of Sirdar Snuggly Baby Bamboo DK in colour A – Cream (shade 131)
3[3:4:4] balls in colour B – Pink (shade 134)
2[2:3:3] balls in colour C – Cherry Red (shade 126)

Hooks:
3.00mm (UK 11) crochet hook
3.50mm (UK 9) crochet hook
4.00mm (UK 8) crochet hook

Tension:
20 sts and 22 rows measure 10cm (4in) square over patt on 4.00mm (UK 8) hook
IT IS ESSENTIAL TO WORK TO THE STATED TENSION TO ACHIEVE SUCCESS

What you have to do:
Work throughout in spike-stitch pattern using main colour for double crochet rows and contrast colour for spike-stitch rows. Work into back loop of each stitch throughout. Shape armholes, neckline and sleeves as directed. Work double crochet border in second contrast colour around neck, lower edge and sleeves. Trim centre front of neck border with a crochet bow.

The Yarn
Sirdar Snuggly Baby Bamboo DK (approx. 95m/104 yards per 50g/1¾oz ball) is 80% bamboo sourced viscose and 20% wool. It makes an attractive machine-washable fabric and there is a good colour choice.

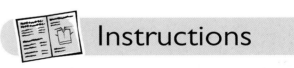

Instructions

BACK:
With 4.00mm (UK 8) hook and A, make 86[92:98:104]ch. Work into back loop of each st throughout.
Foundation row: (RS) 1dc into 2nd ch from hook, 1dc into each ch to end, turn. 85[91:97:103] sts.
Next row: 1ch (does not count as a st), 1dc into each dc to end, turn. Rep last row 6 times more.
Cont in patt as foll:
1st row: (RS) With B, 1ch, 1dc into each of first 3dc, spike st into next dc 2 rows below, *1dc into each of next 5dc, spike st into next dc 2 rows below, rep from *

Abbreviations:

ch = chain
cm = centimetre(s)
cont = continue
dc = double crochet
dc2tog = (insert hook in next st, yrh and draw a loop through) twice, yrh and draw through all 3 loops on hook
foll = follow(s)(ing)
inc = increas(e)(ed)(ing)
patt = pattern
rem = remaining
rep = repeat
RS = right side
spike st = missing next st, insert hook into corresponding st but 2 rows below and work 1 dc as normal
ss = slip stitch
st(s) = stitch(es)
WS = wrong side
yrh = yarn round hook

Note:

When changing colour, always introduce new colour on last part of last stitch in old colour.

to last 3dc, 1 dc into each dc to end, turn. Fasten off.
2nd–8th rows: With A, work 7 rows in dc. Fasten off.
9th row: With B, 1 ch, 1 dc into each of first 6dc, spike st into next dc 2 rows below, *1 dc into each of next 5dc, spike st into next dc 2 rows below, rep from * to last 6dc, 1 dc into each dc to end, turn. Fasten off.
10th–16th rows: With A, work 7 rows in dc. Fasten off.

These 16 rows form patt. Work a further 22[22:26:26] rows in patt, ending with a 6th[6th:10th:10th] patt row.

Shape armholes:

Next row: (RS) With A, ss into each of first 8 sts, 1 ch, 1 dc into each st to last 8 sts, turn. 69[75:81:87] sts.
Keeping patt correct, cont straight for a further 29[29:33:33] rows, ending with a 4th[4th:12th:12th] patt row.

Shape neck:

Keeping patt correct, cont as foll:
Next row: 1 ch, 1 dc into each of first 14[14:16:18] sts, dc2tog over next 2 sts, turn and complete this side of neck first.
Next row: 1 ch, dc2tog over first 2 sts, patt to end, turn.
Next row: 1 ch, patt to last 2 sts, dc2tog over last 2 sts, turn. Rep last 2 rows 3 times more. 7[7:9:11] sts. Patt 6 rows straight. Fasten off.
With RS of work facing, miss 37[43:45:47] sts at centre neck, rejoin A to next st, 1 ch, dc2tog over first 2 sts, patt to end, turn. Complete to match first side of neck.

FRONT:

Work as given for Back.

SLEEVES: (make 2)

With 4.00mm (UK 8) hook and A, make 62[62:68:68]ch. Work foundation row and 1 row in dc as given for Back.

61[61:67:67] sts.

Inc row: 1ch, 2dc into first dc, patt to last dc, 2dc into last dc, turn. 1 st inc at each end of row.

Cont in dc, work 5 more rows, inc 1 st at each end of last row. 65[65:71:71] sts. Cont in patt as foll:

1st row: (RS) With B, 1ch, 1dc into each of first 5dc, *spike st into next dc 2 rows below, 1dc into each of next 5dc, rep from * to end, turn. Fasten off. Change to A.

2nd–4th rows: Work in dc.

5th row: 1ch, 2dc into first dc, 1dc into each dc to last st, 2dc into last st, turn.

6th–8th rows: Work in dc. Fasten off.

9th row: With B, 1dc into each of first 3 sts, *spike st into next dc 2 rows below, 1dc into each of next 5dc, rep from * to last 4 sts, spike st into next dc 2 rows below, 1dc into each of last 3 sts, turn. Fasten off. Change to A.

10th row: As 5th row.

11th–14th rows: Work in dc.

15th row: As 5th row.

16th row: Work in dc. Fasten off. Keeping patt correct, inc 1 st at each end of 4th and every foll 5th row until there are 83[83:89:89] sts. Patt 10 rows straight, ending with 7 rows in A. Fasten off.

 Making up

Join shoulder seams. Sew sleeves into armholes, sewing sides of last 9 rows at top of sleeves to sts left at underarms. Join side and sleeve seams.

Neck border:
Work into back loop only of each st.
With 4.00mm (UK 8) hook and RS of work facing, join A to one shoulder seam and work 1ch, 1dc into each row-end and each dc all around neck edge, join with a ss into first dc. Change to 3.50mm (UK 9) hook and work 3 rounds in dc. Change to 3.00mm (UK 11) hook and work 1 more round in dc. Fasten off.

Lower border:
With 4.00mm (UK 8) hook and RS of work facing, join C to one side seam and work 1ch, 1dc into each st around lower edge, join with a ss into first dc. Work 7 rounds in dc working into back loop only of each st. Fasten off.

Sleeve borders:
With 4.00mm (UK 8) hook and RS of work facing, join C to sleeve seam and work 1ch, 1dc into each st around cuff edge, join with a ss into first dc. Work 3 rounds in dc working into back loop only of each st. Fasten off.

Bow:
With 4.00mm (UK 8) hook and C, make 92ch.

Foundation row: 1dc into 2nd ch from hook, 1dc into each ch to end. 91dc. Fasten off.

Working into other side of foundation ch, join C at centre, 1ch, 1dc into each ch to last ch, 2dc into last ch, 1dc into end of foundation row, working into back loop only, work 2dc into first dc of foundation row, 1dc into each dc to last dc, 2dc into last dc, 1dc into end of foundation row, 2dc into first of foundation ch, 1dc into each of rem ch, join with a ss into first dc. Fasten off.

Make 11ch for knot, 1dc into 2nd ch from hook, 1dc into each ch to end, turn. Work 1 row dc into back loop only of each st. Fasten off.

Fold long strip into a bow shape, wrap knot around centre of bow and sew securely at back. Sew bow to front of neck border.

Cobweb throw

Re-create the elegance of a bygone era with this delicate square-motif throw.

Fine, natural yarn and large openwork squares, which are joined as you work, plus a complementary edging, make an exquisite accessory for a traditional drawing room.

The Yarn

Artesano Alpaca 4 Ply (approx. 184m/201 yards per 50g/1¾oz ball) contains 100% superfine Peruvian alpaca. Its fine quality and naturally slightly brushed appearance are ideal for this fluid, openwork pattern. It is hand wash only. In addition to natural shades like this one there are plenty of bright colours.

GETTING STARTED

 *Individual motifs are not complicated but joining motifs as you work takes concentration.*

Size:
Approximately 110 x 135cm (43 x 53in)

How much yarn:
7 x 50g (1¾oz) hanks of Artesano Alpaca 4 ply in Biscuit (shade SFN21)

Hook:
3.50mm (UK 9) crochet hook

Tension:
Each square measures approximately 25cm (10in) on 3.50mm (UK 9) hook

IT IS ESSENTIAL TO WORK TO THE STATED TENSION TO ACHIEVE SUCCESS

What you have to do:
Work first square to final round as circular motif in rounds with solid centre and chain arches. Transform into square motif on final round by working series of chain arches decorated with picot points and double and triple treble clusters at each corner. Join each square to previous one through picot points on final round as you are working.

Instructions

Abbreviations:

ch = chain(s)

dc = double crochet

dtr3tog = into st indicated work:*yrh twice, insert hook in st, yrh and draw a loop through, (yrh and draw through first 2 loops) twice, rep from * twice more, yrh and draw through all 4 loops

foll = follows

htr = half treble

rep = repeat

RS = right side

sp = space

ss = slip stitch

st(s) = stitch(es)

tr = treble

tr-tr = triple treble

tr-tr3tog = into st indicated work: *yrh 3 times, insert hook in next st, yrh and draw a loop through, (yrh and draw through first 2 loops) 3 times, rep from * twice more, yrh and draw through all 4 loops

yrh = yarn round hook

1ST ROW:
1st square:

With 3.50mm (UK 9) hook make 6ch, join with a ss into first ch to form a ring.

1st round: 3ch (counts 1tr), 11tr into ring, join with a ss into 3rd of 3ch. 12 sts.

2nd round: 3ch, 1tr into st at base of ch, 2tr into each st to end, join with a ss into 3rd of 3ch. 24 sts.

3rd round: 4ch (counts as 1tr, 1ch), (1tr into next tr, 1ch) 23 times, join with a ss into 3rd of 4ch.

4th round: Ss into first 1ch sp, 3ch, 1tr into same sp, 1ch, (2tr into next 1ch sp, 1ch) 23 times, join with a ss into 3rd of 3ch.

5th round: Ss into next 1ch sp, 6ch (counts as 1tr, 3ch), (miss 2tr, 1tr into next 1ch sp, 3ch) 23 times, join with a ss into 3rd of 6ch.

6th round: Ss to centre of first 3ch arch, 1ch, 1dc into same arch, *4ch, 1dc into next 3ch arch, rep from * all round, omitting dc at end of last rep and joining with a ss into first dc.
24 ch arches.

7th round: Ss to centre of first 4ch arch, 1ch, 1dc into same arch, *5ch, 1dc into next 4ch arch, rep from * all round, omitting dc at end of last rep and joining with a ss into first dc.

8th round: Ss to centre of first 5ch arch, 1ch, 1dc into same arch, *6ch, 1dc into next 5ch arch, rep from * all round, omitting dc at end of last rep and joining with a ss into first dc.

9th round: Ss to centre of first 6ch arch, 1ch, 1dc into same arch, *6ch, 1dc into

next 6ch arch, rep from * all round, omitting dc at end of last rep and joining with a ss into first dc.

10th round: Ss to centre of first 6ch arch, 1ch, 1dc into same arch, *7ch, 1dc into next 6ch arch, rep from * all round, omitting dc at end of last rep and joining with a ss into first dc.

11th round: Ss to centre of first 7ch arch, 1ch, 1dc into same arch, *8ch, 1dc into next 7ch arch, rep from * all round, omitting dc at end of last rep and joining with a ss into first dc.

12th round: Ss to centre of first 8ch arch, 1ch, 1dc into same arch, *10ch, 1dc into next 8ch arch, rep from * all round, omitting dc at end of last rep and joining with a ss into first dc.

13th round: Ss to centre of first 10ch arch, 1ch, 1dc into same arch, *12ch, 1dc into next 10ch arch, rep from * to last 10ch arch, 6ch, join by working 1tr-tr into first dc.

14th round: 1ch, 1dc in arch created by last tr-tr, 9ch, 1dc into next 12ch arch, 5ch, ss into side of last dc, *9ch, 1dc into next 12ch arch, 5ch, ss into side of last dc, 4ch, dtr3tog into next dc, 4ch, tr-tr3tog into same dc, 5ch, ss into top of tr-tr3tog, 4ch, dtr3tog into same dc, 4ch, 1dc into next 12ch arch, 5ch, ss into side of last dc**, (9ch, 1dc into next 12ch arch, 5ch, ss into side of last dc) 4 times, rep from * 3 times more, ending last rep at **, (9ch, 1dc into next 12ch arch, 5ch, ss into side of last dc) twice, 9ch, join with a ss into first dc, 5ch, ss into same place as last ss. Fasten off.

2nd square:
Work 13 rounds as given for 1st square.
Now join 2 squares together through 5ch picots on 14th round as foll:

14th round: 1ch, 1dc into arch created by last tr-tr, 9ch, 1dc into next 12ch arch, 5ch, ss into side of last dc, *9ch, 1dc into next 12ch arch, 5ch, ss into side of last dc, 4ch, dtr3tog into next dc, 4ch, tr-tr3tog into same dc**, 5ch, ss into top of tr-tr3tog, 4ch, dtr3tog into same dc, 4ch, 1dc into next 12ch arch, 5ch, ss into side of last dc, (9ch, 1dc into next 12ch arch, 5ch, ss into side of last dc) 4 times, rep from * once more, then from * to ** again, 5ch, insert hook from back to front through 5ch picot at top of one corner tr-tr3tog on 1st square and pull loop through picot and loop on hook, ss into top of working tr-tr3tog, 4ch, dtr3tog into same dc, 4ch, 1dc into next 12ch arch, 5ch, insert hook from back to front through next 5ch picot on 1st square and pull loop through picot and loop on hook, ss into side of last dc, (9ch, 1dc into next 12ch arch, 5ch, insert hook from back

to front through next 5ch picot on 1st square and pull loop through picot and loop on hook, ss into side of last dc) 5 times, 4ch, dtr3tog into next dc, 4ch, tr-tr3tog into same dc, 5ch, insert hook from back to front through 5ch picot at corner of 1st square and pull loop through picot and loop on hook, ss into top of working tr-tr3tog, 4ch, dtr3tog into same dc, 4ch, 1dc into next 12ch arch, 5ch, ss into side of last dc, (9ch, 1dc into next 12ch arch, 5ch, ss into side of last dc) twice, 9ch, join with a ss into first dc, 5ch, ss into same place as last ss. Fasten off. Work 2 more squares joining each one to previous square on the final round as given for 2nd square.

2ND, 3RD, 4TH AND 5TH ROWS:
1st square:
Work 13 rounds as given for 1st square on 1st row. Join to bottom of 1st square on row above through 5ch picots as given for 14th round of 2nd square on 1st row.

2nd square:
Work 13 rounds as given for 1st square on 1st row. Join to bottom of 2nd square on row above and side of 1st square on same row through corresponding 5ch picots on each square. Join a further 2 squares on to row in same way.

EDGING:
With 3.50mm (UK 9) hook and RS of work facing, join yarn to 5ch picot at one corner.

1st round: 1ch, 1dc into same picot, *9ch, 1dc into next picot, rep from * all round outer edge of throw, join with a ss into first dc.

2nd round: 1ch, 1dc into st at base of join, *6ch, 1dc into next 9ch arch, 6ch, 1dc into next dc, rep from * all round, omitting dc at end of last rep, join with a ss into first dc.

3rd round: Ss to centre of first 6ch arch, 1ch, 1dc into same arch, *6ch, 1dc into next 6ch arch, rep from * , ending last rep with 3ch, join by working 1tr into first dc.

4th round: 1ch, 1dc into arch created by last tr, 3ch, 1dc into next 6ch arch, *3ch, (1dc, 1htr, 3tr, 1htr, 1dc) into next 6ch arch, 3ch, 1dc into next 6ch arch, rep from * to end, join with a ss into first dc. Fasten off.

Circus squares cushion

Choose ultra-bright colours for a zingy statement cushion.

GETTING STARTED

Working granny squares is easy but attention to detail is needed for a neat finish.

Size:
To fit a 40cm (16in) square cushion pad

How much yarn:
1 x 50g (1¾oz) ball of King Cole Merino Blend DK in each of six colours: A – Scarlet (shade 9); B – Copper (shade 109); C – Corn (shade 794); D – Linden (shade 165); E – Turquoise (shade 18) and F – Bluebell (shade 26)

Hooks:
3.50mm (UK 9) crochet hook
4.00mm (UK 8) crochet hook

Additional items:
35cm (14in) or 40cm (16in) red zip fastener
Red sewing thread and needle
40cm (16in) square cushion pad

Tension:
First square measures 13.5 x 13.5cm (5¼ x 5¼in) on 4.00mm (UK 8) hook
IT IS ESSENTIAL TO WORK TO THE STATED TENSION TO ACHIEVE SUCCESS

What you have to do:
Make eight granny squares, working each round in a different colour as directed. Sew four squares together for front and remaining four squares together for back. Work border around front and back in colours as directed. Crochet back and front together. Sew in zip fastener.

The Yarn
King Cole Merino Blend DK (approx. 112m/122 yards per 50g/1¾oz ball) contains 100% pure new wool in a practical machine-washable format. There is a fantastic range of colours.

Granny squares in a large selection of bright shades are sewn together and then bordered with more rounds to produce a cushion cover that is as bright as a circus parade.

 Instructions

SQUARES:
Make 8 squares in all, working each round in a different colour as shown here:

1st square:
1st round: E; **2nd round:** B; **3rd round:** F; **4th round:** A; **5th round:** D; **6th round:** B.

2nd square:
1st round: A; **2nd round:** D; **3rd round:** C; **4th round:** F; **5th round:** E; **6th round:** B.

3rd square:
1st round: B; **2nd round:** D; **3rd round:** A; **4th round:** E; **5th round:** C; **6th round:** B.

4th square:
1st round: D; **2nd round:** A; **3rd round:** E; **4th round:** C; **5th round:** F; **6th round:** B.

5th square:
1st round: E; **2nd round:** B; **3rd round:** D; **4th round:** C; **5th round:** A; **6th round:** F.

6th square:
1st round: C; **2nd round:** E; **3rd round:** A;

Abbreviations:

ch = chain
cm = centimetre(s)
dc = double crochet
rep = repeat
RS = right side
sp(s) = space(s)
ss = slip stitch
st(s) = stitch(es)
tr = treble
WS = wrong side

Note: As you work squares, some tails can be enclosed by next round of sts to avoid sewing in later.

4th round: D; **5th round:** B; **6th round:** F.

7th square:

1st round: A; **2nd round:** F; **3rd round:** B;
4th round: E; **5th round:** C; **6th round:** F.

8th square:

1st round: F; **2nd round:** C; **3rd round:** E;
4th round: A; **5th round:** D; **6th round:** F.

FIRST SQUARE:

With 4.00mm (UK 8) hook and first colour, make 12ch, join with a ss in first ch to form a ring.

1st round: 3ch (counts as first tr), 2tr in ring, (1ch, 3tr in ring) 7 times, 1ch, join with a ss in 3rd of 3ch. Fasten off. 8 groups of 3tr.

2nd round: Join next colour to any 1ch sp, 3ch, 2tr in same sp, (1ch, 3tr in next 1ch sp) 7 times, 1ch, join with a ss in 3rd of 3ch. Fasten off. 8 groups.

3rd round: Join next colour to any 1ch sp, 3ch, (2tr, 1ch, 3tr) in same sp, *1ch, (3tr, 1ch, 3tr) in next 1ch sp, rep from * 6 more times, 1ch, join with a ss in 3rd of 3ch. Fasten off. 16 groups.

4th round: Join next colour to any 1ch sp between any 2 groups worked in same place, 3ch, (2tr, 1ch, 3tr)

in same sp, *(1ch, 3tr in next 1ch sp) 3 times, 1ch, (3tr, 1ch, 3tr) in next 1ch sp, rep from * twice more, (1ch, 3tr in next 1ch sp) 3 times, 1ch, join with a ss in 3rd of 3ch. Fasten off. 20 groups.

5th round: Join next colour to any 1ch sp between 2 groups at any corner, 3ch, (2tr, 1ch, 3tr) in same sp, *(1ch, 3tr in next 1ch sp) 4 times, 1ch, (3tr, 1ch, 3tr) in next 1ch sp, rep from * twice more, (1ch, 3tr in next 1ch sp) 4 times, 1ch, join with a ss in 3rd of 3ch. Fasten off. 24 groups.

6th round: Join next colour to 1ch sp at any corner, 2ch, 1dc in same sp, *1dc in each tr and ch sp to next corner, (1dc, 1ch, 1dc) in ch sp at corner, rep from * twice more, 1dc in each tr and ch sp to corner, join with a ss in first of 2ch. Fasten off, leaving a 25cm (10in) tail. 25dc on each side.

Work 2nd–8th squares as First square.

FRONT:

Using a flat seam, join 1st–4th squares into a larger square in foll order: 1st square, top left; 2nd square, top right; 3rd square, lower left and 4th square, lower right.

Border:

1st round: With 4.00mm (UK 8) hook and RS of work

facing, join B to 1ch sp at one corner, 2ch, 1dc in same sp, *1dc in each of 25dc, 1dc in seam, 1dc in each of 25dc, (1dc, 1ch, 1dc) in 1ch sp at next corner, rep from * twice more, 1dc in each of 25dc, 1dc in seam, 1dc in each of 25dc, join with a ss in first of 2ch.

2nd round: Ss in 1ch sp, 3ch, 1dc in same sp, *1dc in each of 53dc, (1dc, 2ch, 1dc) in 1ch sp at corner, rep from * twice more, 1dc in each of 53dc, join with a ss in first of 3ch. Fasten off. 55dc on each side and 2ch at each corner.

3rd round: Join D to 2ch sp at any corner, 3ch, (2tr, 1ch, 3tr) in same sp, *(1ch, miss 3dc, 3tr in next dc) 13 times, 1ch, miss 3dc, (3tr, 1ch, 3tr) in 2ch sp at corner, rep from * twice more, (1ch, miss 3dc, 3tr in next dc) 13 times, 1ch, join with a ss in 3rd of 3ch. Fasten off.

4th round: Join C to 1ch sp at any corner, 3ch, (2tr, 1ch, 3tr) in same sp, *(1ch, 3tr in next 1ch sp) 14 times, 1ch, (3tr, 1ch, 3tr) in 1ch sp at corner, rep from * twice more, (1ch, 3tr in next 1ch sp) 14 times, 1ch, join with a ss in 3rd of 3ch. Fasten off.

5th round: Join E to 1ch sp at any corner, 3ch, (2tr, 1ch, 3tr) in same sp, *(1ch, 3tr in next 1ch sp) 15 times, 1ch, (3tr, 1ch, 3tr) in 1ch sp at corner, rep from * twice more, (1ch, 3tr in next 1ch sp) 15 times, 1ch, join with a ss in 3rd of 3ch. Fasten off.

6th round: Join A to 1ch sp at any corner, 3ch, 1dc in same sp, *1dc in each tr and ch sp to corner, (1dc, 2ch, 1dc) in 1ch sp at corner, rep from * twice more, 1dc in each tr and ch sp to corner, join with a ss in first of 3ch. Fasten off.

BACK:
Using a flat seam, join 5th–8th squares into a larger square in foll order: 5th square, top left; 6th square, top right; 7th square, lower left and 8th square, lower right.

Border:
Work as given for Front, using F for 1st and 2nd rounds, B for 3rd round, E for 4th round, C for 5th round and A for 6th round.

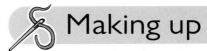 ## Making up

Place Front and Back together with WS facing and using 3.50mm (UK 9) hook, join A to both ch sps at one corner. Working through both thicknesses together: 3ch, 1dc in same place, *1dc in each pair of dc to corner, (1dc, 2ch, 1dc) in both ch sps at corner, rep from * twice more, then work around zip opening: 1dc in each dc of one thickness only to corner, turn and work back along other side of opening. Fasten off.

Pin zip into opening, with crochet edge just clear of teeth on each side. Backstitch zip in place using red sewing thread. If necessary, join a few sts of crochet at each end of zip for a neat finish.

Pineapple doily

Proof that a classic pattern can look contemporary and cool.

This traditional pineapple doily is easier to crochet than it may appear. Start by working in the round, and then complete the six pineapples one at a time.

The Yarn

DMC Petra No. 3 (approx. 280m/305 yards per 100g/3½oz ball) is a 100% cotton mercerized thread, perfect for craft items. It produces a soft and supple fabric, and is available in a wide range of pastel colours and strong shades.

GETTING STARTED

 This stunning doily is both quick and easy to make.

Size:

Doily measures 32cm (12½in) in diameter

How much yarn:

1 x 100g (3½oz) ball of DMC Petra No 3 in White (shade B5200)

Hook:

2.00mm (UK 14) crochet hook

Tension:

First 3 rounds measure 6.5cm (2½in) over patt on 2.00mm (UK 14) hook
IT IS ESSENTIAL TO WORK TO THE STATED TENSION TO ACHIEVE SUCCESS

What you have to do:

Work in rounds of trebles, then simple shell pattern. Begin pineapple motifs still working in rounds. Complete each pineapple separately incorporating spiked edging.

Instructions

Abbreviations:

ch = chain
cm = centimetre(s)
dc = double crochet
dtr = double treble
patt = pattern
rep = repeat
RS = right side
sp(s) = space(s)
ss = slip stitch
st(s) = stitch(es)
tr = treble
yrh = yarn round hook

DOILY:

With 2.00mm (UK 14) hook make 11ch, join with a ss in first ch to form a ring.

1st round: 3ch (counts as first tr), 23tr in ring, join with a ss in 3rd of 3ch. 24 sts.

2nd round: 3ch, 1tr in same place as ss, (3ch, miss 1tr, 2tr in next tr) 11 times, 3ch, miss last tr; join with a ss in 3rd of 3ch. Twelve 3ch sps.

3rd round: Ss in next tr and in first ch sp, 3ch, (1tr, 2ch, 2tr) in same ch sp as last ss*, (2tr, 2ch, 2tr) – called 1 shell – in each ch sp, join with a ss in 3rd of 3ch.

4th round: Work as 3rd round to *, (1ch, 1 shell) in 2ch sp at centre of each shell, 1ch, join with a ss in 3rd of 3ch.

5th round: Work as 3rd round to *,

First pineapple:

1st row: (RS) With RS facing, rejoin yarn to 2ch sp at centre of any shell on 10th round, (3ch, 1tr, 2ch, 2tr) in same 2ch sp, 3ch, miss next 3ch sp, (1dc in next 3ch sp, 3ch) 7 times, 1 shell in 2ch sp at centre of next shell on 10th round (note: this 2ch sp is joining point for next pineapple), turn.

2nd row: Ss in each of first 2tr and in 2ch sp, (3ch, 1tr, 2ch, 2tr) in same 2ch sp*, 3ch, miss next 3ch sp, (1dc in next 3ch sp, 3ch) 6 times, 1 shell in 2ch sp at centre of shell, turn.

3rd row: Work as given for 2nd row working instructions in brackets 5 times not 6.

4th row: Work as given for 2nd row working instructions in brackets 4 times not 6.

5th row: Work as given for 2nd row working instructions in brackets 3 times not 6.

6th row: Work as given for 2nd row working instructions in brackets 2 times not 6.

7th row: Work as given for 2nd row to *, 3ch, miss next 3ch sp, 1dc in next 3ch sp, 3ch, 1 shell in 2ch sp at centre of shell, turn.

8th row: Work as given for 2nd row to *, 1 shell in 2ch sp at centre of shell, turn.

9th row: Ss in each of first 2tr and in 2ch sp, 3ch, leaving last loop of each tr on hook work 1tr in same 2ch sp as last ss and 2tr in 2ch sp at centre of next shell, yrh and draw through all 4 loops.
Fasten off.

2nd to 6th pineapples:

With RS facing, rejoin yarn to 10th round in the 2ch sp at centre of same shell as shell at end of 1st row of previous pineapple was worked. Work as 1st pineapple noting that 2nd shell of 1st row of 6th pineapple is worked in centre of same shell as first shell of 1st pineapple.

Darn in all ends. Pin out and press under a damp cloth.

(2ch, 1 shell) in 2ch sp at centre of each shell, 2ch, join with a ss in 3rd of 3ch.

6th round: Ss in next tr and in first 2ch sp, (3ch, 1tr, 5ch, 2tr) in same ch sp as last ss, *4ch, miss next 2ch sp, 1 shell in 2ch sp at centre of next shell, 4ch, miss next 2ch sp, (2tr, 5ch, 2tr) in 2ch sp at centre of next shell, rep from * 4 times more, 4ch, miss next 2ch sp, 1 shell in 2ch sp at centre of last shell, 4ch, miss last 2ch sp, join with a ss in 3rd of 3ch.

7th round: Ss in next tr and in 5ch sp, 4ch (counts as first dtr), 10dtr in same 5ch sp, (3ch, 1 shell in 2ch sp at centre of next shell, 3ch, 11dtr in 5ch sp) 5 times, 3ch, 1 shell in 2ch sp at centre of next shell, 3ch, join with a ss in 4th of 4ch.

8th round: Ss in next dtr, 5ch (counts as 1dtr and 1ch), 1dtr in next dtr, (1ch, 1dtr) in each of next 8dtr, *3ch, 1 shell in 2ch sp at centre of next shell, 3ch, miss next dtr, 1dtr in next dtr, (1ch, 1dtr) in each of next 9dtr, rep from * 4 times more, 3ch, 1 shell in 2ch sp at centre of next shell, 3ch, join with a ss in 4th of 5ch.

9th round: 1ch (does not count as a st), *(1dc in next 1ch sp, 3ch) 9 times, 1 shell in 2ch sp at centre of next shell, 3ch, rep from * 5 times more, join with a ss in first dc.

10th round: 1ch, *(1dc in next 3ch sp, 3ch) 8 times, 1 shell in 2ch sp at centre of next shell, 3ch, miss next 3ch sp, rep from * 5 times more, join with a ss in first dc.
Fasten off.

Index

Acknowledgements

Managing Editor: Clare Churly
Editors: Lesley Malkin and Eleanor van Zandt
Senior Art Editor: Juliette Norsworthy
Designer: Janis Utton
Production Controller: Sarah Kramer